P9-DDM-889

Listening to Conflict

Listening to Conflict

Finding Constructive Solutions to Workplace Disputes

Erik J. Van Slyke

AMACOM
American Management Association

New York • Boston • Chicago • Kansas City • San Francisco • Washington, D.C.
Brussels • Mexico City • Tokyo • Toronto

This publication is designed to provide accurate and authoritative information in regard to the subject matter covered. It is sold with the understanding that the publisher is not engaged in rendering legal, accounting, or other professional service. If legal advice or other expert assistance is required, the services of a competent professional person should be sought.

Library of Congress Cataloging-in-Publication Data

Van Slyke, Erik J.
    Listening to conflict : finding constructive solutions to workplace disputes / Erik J. Van Slyke.
       p.   cm.
    Includes index.
    ISBN 0-8144-0429-4
    1. Conflict management.   2. Problem solving.   I. Title.
HD42.V36   1999
658.4'053—dc21   98-31116
                                                     CIP

Printing number

10 9 8 7 6 5 4 3 2 1

*For **Terri**, who always listens*

Contents

Preface

Whether we are in conflict with another party or mediating a dispute between two parties, the first step we often take toward resolution is to offer additional information intended to demonstrate the logic and reasoning that supports our view of a fair solution. When the parties remain unconvinced, we typically provide further amplification of the position already rejected by those in dissension. When this fails, we persuade, cajole, argue, manipulate, sulk, bully, stamp our feet, arbitrate, or withdraw from the interaction. Very often, this process proves time-consuming and frustrating, and the conflict ends without a satisfactory resolution. We walk away from the interaction thinking, "Why don't they listen to me?"

Exactly.

Listening is the key to constructive conflict resolution. The problem in conflict, however, is not whether the other party listens to us, but rather whether we listen to and understand the other party's perspective. Only after we have listened to the other party will that party want to listen to us. Only after the other party feels understood will he or she want to understand and be influenced by us.

When we begin the resolution process by listening, we create an environment that demonstrates a desire for constructive resolution. We allow the other party to communicate its needs, interests, and ideas—both what that party knows and what it may not yet understand. This reduces the chance that personality differences will interfere with constructive problem-solving and provides information that will help us understand how to seek resolution. We are given a clear picture of the other party's inner motivations, agendas, and objectives that will help us create solutions that satisfy the interests of both parties.

The environment created by listening is especially effective when we are working to resolve the conflicts of others. As supervisors, team leaders, and human resources professionals, we are often asked—or compelled—to referee disputes between employees, coworkers, customers, suppliers, and even senior managers. The tools of collaborative resolution establish our position as an objective mediator, guide the parties toward constructive solutions, and build relationships that prevent future conflicts from deteriorating into destructive disagreements. In addition, the listening-based approach to conflict resolution ensures that we develop organization cultures that embrace and nurture the productive aspects of conflict.

In order to use listening as a tool for constructive resolution, we must develop five important areas of understanding:

1. The factors that influence conflict
2. Self-awareness
3. Self-mastery
4. Empathic listening skills
5. The six steps of collaborative conflict resolution

This book provides a comprehensive overview of conflict resolution and demonstrates how listening can open pathways to understanding and constructive solutions. It takes an inside-out approach to the resolution process and suggests that we cannot resolve the disputes we have with others until we resolve the conflicts within ourselves. In other words, we cannot listen to and understand another party until we know how to listen to and understand ourselves. Self-awareness lays the foundation for self-mastery, and self-mastery lays the foundation for productive relationships with others.

Chapter 1 provides a definition of conflict and an overview of the factors that influence the resolution process. It examines how these factors shape our perceptions and create barriers to constructive interaction.

Before we can improve our skills, however, we must become aware of our preexisting orientations and the obstacles they may present. Chapter 2 helps us understand and develop the self awareness to establish effective working relationships with others. It explores our interpersonal preferences and explains how these preferences influence our perceptions and resulting behavior during a dispute.

Chapter 3 explains how self-awareness can lead to self-mastery and change the action-reaction cycle that leads to destructive conflict resolution. It provides four important guiding principles that can be used to shape our own behavior as well as the behavior of others. These principles also help us sustain our approach to conflict resolution in spite of the interpersonal and situational constraints that may influence our approach.

Chapter 4 identifies the six levels of listening and teaches empathic listening techniques and methods. It outlines the important role of empathy in conveying understanding and creating an environment that encourages open communication. The chapter shows how listening breaks the cycle of destructive conflict and provides the tools to explore the options for constructive resolution.

Chapter 5 provides a framework for conflict resolution and demonstrates how to apply the principles and tools learned in the previous chapters. In particular, it demonstrates where listening fits into the formal steps of collaborative resolution and how to achieve consensus solutions.

The final two chapters expand upon the five areas of understanding required for constructive resolution. Chapter 6 provides two important tools that are used to establish a collaborative environment and explores the solutions to some commonly encountered challenges to the Listening to Conflict approach. Chapter 7 proposes that organizations need to create cultures of constructive conflict to maintain competitive advantage, and outlines the requirements for teaching collaborative conflict resolution.

As you read this book, take time to reflect on and analyze your personal situation and the conflicts you encounter. Try to see how the techniques and methods discussed might influence the interactions. If you identify a conflict that is of relatively low intensity, practice the skills in that situation. If your conflicts are more intense and upsetting, enlist the help of family, friends, or coworkers to role-play with you until you build your confidence. Be patient and forgiving with yourself. Improving and maintaining these skills is a lifelong process that requires practice, effort, and attention. Every conflict provides a new opportunity to refine these skills and learn how to make the next interaction more positive.

Reading this book is the first step toward improving your ability to manage and resolve conflict constructively. The next step is up to you.

Acknowledgments

I listened to many people in the process of writing this book, and I am thankful for their encouragement and support.

I am deeply indebted to the many scholars whose work laid the foundations on which this project is based. I am especially grateful to the individuals, clients, and students who asked questions and shared experiences that inspired my interest, research, and thoughts. Special thanks go to Roger and Sandy Plachy of the Job Results Management Institute for encouraging me to walk this path and for serving as role models, both professionally and personally; Cindy Sherwood for her valuable guidance, spirit, and endorsement; Hanna Sano for her wit, wisdom, and resources; Dennis McKnight for continuing to share his insights; Debra DeMeis and Charles Temple of Hobart and William Smith Colleges for teaching me the fundamentals of human development; Debra Shapiro of the Kenan-Flaglar Business School at the University of North Carolina for sparking my interest in negotiation and conflict management; Suzanne Isaack for her enthusiastic analysis and suggestions; Niels Bucooem and Barbara Horowitn for their invaluable recommendations for improving the manuscript; Adrienne Hickey, my AMACOM editor, for her endorsement, insight, commitment, and incredible patience; Bud and Marilyn Van Slyke, my parents, for instilling the Principles of Interaction throughout my life; and Terri, my best friend and wife, who listened as I read the book aloud and who provided the support, encouragement, and space I needed to complete the project.

1

Understanding Conflict

"Warfare is the greatest affair of state, the basis of life and death, the Way (Tao) to survival or extinction. It must be thoroughly pondered and analyzed."

Sun-tzu, *The Art of War*

Not long ago, a manager described a frustrating situation that she was trying to understand. Approximately three years earlier she had hired a bright recent graduate of a top MBA program to work in her accounting and finance department. He had terrific work experience and great recommendations, and he seemed eager to dive in and learn. Once he was hired, his self-effacing, charming personality helped him immediately establish good working relationships with his coworkers, and he proved to be a quick study and a hard worker. Within the first few months, he even made some improvements to important management reports that caught the attention of the department vice president.

However, a turning point occurred six months into his tenure with the organization, at the time of his first performance appraisal. The first step in the organization's appraisal process was for the employee to complete a self-assessment and submit it to the manager. The manager and employee then would discuss the employee's self-assessment, and the manager would add his or her thoughts before they agreed on a final version. The final version was then submitted to human resources.

When the manager received a copy of her employee's assessment, she was shocked. He severely criticized her and the department. He complained that she lacked vision, did not communicate her expectations clearly, and ignored his knowledge and capabilities. He felt that while he performed at the "A" level on the appraisal, his performance rating was inflated, since he was given only lower-level assignments. He claimed that others in the department dragged their feet on assignments and that they were not held accountable for their work. He ended by saying that he hoped they could establish an action plan to remedy the unsatisfactory situation. Not surprisingly, the manager revealed, the subsequent appraisal conversation was strained, and she remained dumbfounded about the shift in her employee's attitude.

During the next few months, she observed the employee becoming progressively more argumentative not only with her, but also with his coworkers. He frequently questioned decisions and presented recommendations that were contrary to department standards and procedures. While he completed assignments on time, they often contained careless errors and omissions. When she tried to confront him about the change in his attitude and performance, the conversations were difficult and left her exhausted. She even solicited the help of other managers and human resources, but with no favorable results. After fourteen months of employment, she fired him.

Many months later, when the manager attended a professional association meeting, she heard that the same employee had been working for a competitor for over a year. Not only had he received a fast promotion to a management position, but he also was considered one of that company's up-and-comers. She was delighted for his success, but as she thought back on her interaction with him, she also was disappointed. She questioned her inability to manage the conflict with him effectively. And she wondered what more she could have done to maintain the relationship and make the situation productive for both of them.

This manager's story is probably familiar to you. Every day we hear stories of the conflicts in people's lives:

> "This meeting is running late, and it's my turn to pick
> up the kids. It's almost 5:30, and the day-care center

will charge extra if I'm not there by 6:30. I'm trying to make a good impression on my boss by working hard and putting in some extra hours, but I'm afraid he won't think I'm serious about my career if I leave this meeting."

"My wife doesn't seem to care about my opinions or needs. I keep telling her what I want from her, and she agrees at the time. But when push comes to shove, it's as if she forgets we had the conversation."

"The customer was furious when I answered the telephone. After a few expletives, he demanded to speak to a manager because he didn't think that a peon customer service rep making minimum wage knows enough to solve his problem."

"The marketing department has been incredibly unreasonable in the last few New Product Development Team meetings. We are behind schedule in creating the code for this new software product, but the customers keep changing their technical requirements. I don't think the customers really know what they want, and I am not sure that marketing understands our capabilities."

"My teenage daughter is rebellious. No matter what I do, she won't listen to me. I'm only trying to help her."

"Whew! I'm exhausted from the meeting with the union. We've been negotiating for two months, but I think we are finally making progress. It wouldn't surprise me if our final deal were the best ever for both sides."

"Six months ago, I thought I was going to get a divorce. But my husband and I have been in counseling, and we are finally starting to understand each other. We are not out of the woods, but I feel we are closer now than we've been in a long time."

Conflict is a regular part of everyday life. At best, it provides an opportunity to learn and a chance for innovation and change. At worst, it destroys individuals, breaks up families, and halts production within organizations.

Conflict is present in all of our important relationships and can arise in virtually any social setting. It can occur between two or more parties, and it can occur within oneself. Conflict takes place in formal settings across international negotiation tables, and it appears in the informal and personal relationships we have with friends and coworkers.

Very often, we see conflict as negative or destructive. It's a problem in need of a quick fix, or a difficulty to be avoided. Yet this perspective is unsatisfying because we know that sometimes conflict produces good outcomes for all parties involved. When we try to accept conflict as positive and constructive, however, we are left feeling equally unsatisfied. Although it may compel the sharing of information or shed new light on a situation, the resolution process can be stressful and painstaking.

Our view of conflict is determined largely by our ability to achieve a favorable outcome. Do we achieve the result we want? Do we feel as if we made our point or got our way? Is the relationship maintained, or even improved? Has the conflict been resolved? Or has it merely been managed for the short term?

Since conflict is such a common event that often produces important results, our goal as managers, coworkers, and individuals should not be to eliminate it. Instead, we should create an environment that encourages and maintains its positive and productive aspects. Not every conflict can be resolved, but we should at least approach all conflict with a mind-set to seek constructive resolution.

Listening plays a vital role in creating that environment, both personally and organizationally. When we learn how to listen in the face of the most challenging conflicts, we create positive relationship dynamics that foster open communication, acceptance, and trust, the seeds of constructive collaboration. The first step is to develop an understanding of the nature of conflict, why conflict occurs, and the tools required to establish a productive conflict environment.

Definition of Conflict

Conflict is the competition between interdependent parties who perceive that they have incompatible needs, goals, desires, or ideas. It is a situation in which people cannot agree or create harmony with one another. The important elements of this definition are *competition, interdependence,* and *perceived incompatibility.* These three elements provide an initial foundation for understanding the nature of conflict.

Competition

Competition is the process of striving for an objective. This may involve a solitary party striving to achieve a goal, or it may consist of two or more parties acting independently to secure something that only one may possess. If I want to lower my golf handicap by ten strokes, for example, I am striving to achieve a goal and competing against myself or against the benchmark I established. If I want to win the golf tournament, I am competing independently against other golfers who also want to win the match.

During conflict, "winning" is defined by any of a variety of objectives. For example, sometimes the objective might be to "get our way," while other times it might be making sure that other parties "do not get their way." The objective also may be to "restore harmony," in which case it does not matter how the conflict is resolved, so long as the conflict ends. No matter how we define winning in a given conflict, the process of striving to achieve that objective establishes a competitive environment.

Competition, however, is not always conscious and driven by stated objectives. It is often unconscious and hard to detect. When I state that I want to "win" or to "get my way," it is obvious that I am competing. I know it and you know it. But competitiveness is usually less obvious than that. On the surface, it may be displayed as the other party acting stubborn, refusing to participate, or even throwing a temper tantrum. He might try to use his power or authority or call in another party with higher authority. We also may see syrupy smiles, feigned friendship, or pandering politesse. These unconscious behavioral tactics are part of the competitive strategy that each person develops over a lifetime that helps him or her achieve objectives.

Most often, people are unaware of their specific competitive behavior. They just know that it is working and that they are achieving their objective. But sometimes they may be increasingly frustrated because their behavioral strategy is not producing the usual results. In either case, they continue to focus subconsciously on whether they are "winning" or "losing" the conflict competition. They have not said aloud that they want to win, but the process of resolving the dispute becomes a tough competitive battle.

Our competitive behavior has biological origins and is further reinforced by cultural influences. Biologically, competitiveness is an important part of the genetic programming that ensures species survival. Except during the mating season, most animals go about their business without paying much attention to other members of their own species. They establish social systems that prevent the population from exceeding the carrying capacity of the habitat, or they distribute important resources such as food, nest sites, or mates in a systematic way.

In some cases, external agents such as early frost or drought reduce the species population. Other species, however, are subject to population controls that depend on density, and thus the availability of resources. For example, put one pregnant guppy or fifty adults in a five-gallon tank, and in either case, the population will stabilize at about nine. Adults correct the overabundance by fighting and by eating extra offspring.

Other species control population size and density by forcibly excluding certain adults from specific resources. The most common form of the exclusion strategy involves dividing the habitat into defended territories. Each territory, or at least the hotly contested ones, either has a local abundance of the resources necessary for raising offspring or encompasses one of a limited number of favorable breeding sites. Seals, for example, are highly territorial and compete for the limited resource of breeding sites. The best place for these aquatic mammals to mate, give birth, and raise young is a small, secluded beach, inaccessible to both aquatic and terrestrial predators. The males contest vigorously and often fatally for these special places, since controlling one is the only way a male's genes can avoid extinction. These exclusion systems rest on competition for control of the scarce resources that make successful breeding possible for that particular species.

Aggression, the drive to fight and prevail, is a further manifestation of this competitive instinct. It is motivated not by cultural conditioning but by hormones and releasers, and genes have adjusted the programming of aggression to suit the risks and benefits to the species. Sea lions, for example, risk a fight to the death for mating privileges, since failure would be genetic suicide. Mountain sheep, on the other hand, engage in ritual duels from which the loser retires gracefully, in full expectation of better odds in future seasons. Most social systems contain the latter type of encounter, in which well-orchestrated, ritualized restraint ensures that combatants will suffer no serious injury. Many species even have a motor program that serves as a sign stimulus for surrender and instantly limits further aggression. Dogs, for example, expose their most unprotected spot, their bellies. This signals that the contest is over and the competition stops.

Aggression within various species of animals usually lacks the intensity of violence and disruption that we tend to associate with fighting. Fighting, for the most part, is a purposeful ritual. With practically no injury, the animals in a group sort themselves out into a stable social order that establishes a hierarchy, ensures that resources meet the demands of the population, and enhances the group's ability to survive.

Humans, according to Konrad Lorenz, a German ethologist, also are programmed to engage in this form of competition (Lorenz, 1952). Modern society, however, denies us the small groups to which we evolved and thus thwarts our adaptive and restrained aggressive drives. Consequently, he theorizes, humans display their aggressive behavior through such means as intraspecies war and racial conflict. And since these consequences of our unnatural societies are not consistently acceptable, we have also developed alternative ritualized "safety valves," such as sports and hunting, to release the pent-up motivational drives.

Culturally, we further emphasize the biological foundation of competitiveness through a variety of social mechanisms. We place emphasis on games, sports, business market share, and economic, political, and social stratification. Religions claim that they are the "one true faith." We make statements such as, "Winning is important," "You should be proud of beating someone so good," or "You must feel bad since you lost," which reinforce the competitive norm. We also perceive competition as efficient (for economic markets and politics), healthy (for intellectual stimulation and growth), and fun (for leisure and recreation). Much of the literature surrounding conflict resolution even uses competitive terms such as *win, lose, game, strategy,* or *tactics.*

Research data, however, suggest that people achieve more if they work cooperatively with others rather than competitively (Thomas, 1957). In fact, we can readily accept that a competitive job, school, or social situation, where someone wins by making others fail, causes dreadful stress, resentment of the winner, contempt for the losers, low self-esteem, and major barriers to supportive relationships. But collaboration flies in the face of biological and cultural influences. It seems contrary to our nature to be fully cooperative, especially if we are in high conflict with another party. Instead, parties in conflict appear more inclined to interfere with one another's attainment of goals. As each person in the conflict sees the others as increasingly manipulative, controlling, stubborn, or power-hungry, the competitive walls are raised higher, and we prevent ourselves and them from cooperating enough to solve the conflict.

Competition, then, is an important part of the definition of conflict because it describes both the condition that causes conflict and a significant barrier to constructive resolution. Our biological drive was designed to help us acquire our share of the limited resources required for survival. But most of our everyday conflicts are not about dividing scarce resources. Instead, they are about issues that require innovative problem solving or mutual understanding. When we learn how to break down the competitive walls within the other party and ourselves, we will establish an environment with abundant resources for resolution.

Interdependence

The second important element of the definition of conflict is *interdependence*. Interdependence implies that people depend on one another at some level. In the workplace, managers need employees to accomplish results that lead to department or organization success. Likewise, employees need managers to help clarify goals and objectives, give feedback about performance, and provide fair compensation for the work performed. In families and personal relationships, people rely on one another to enhance emotional satisfaction through mutual acceptance, support, encouragement, or love.

When we are in conflict with others, however, we become frustrated by a troublesome dilemma. On the one hand, we realize that our preferred outcome involves the participation of the other parties. We feel *dependent* upon them to satisfy our need, resolve the difference, or provide needed support. On the other hand, we also feel that we would like to eliminate the obstacles—or the people—that stand in our way. We want to get the desired results *independent* of them. We wish we could get what we want through our own effort, or at least exist without this "problem" in our life. Sometimes we do have alternatives that help us avoid the conflict, but we know that over the long term, avoidance does not produce the results we want.

So, we are faced with a dilemma. Our preferred outcome requires a degree of dependence on *them*. It requires their contribution, their input, and their feedback. The preferred way of obtaining the outcome requires independence of *us*. It requires that *I* do it, *I* take responsibility, *I* become self-reliant, and *I* achieve the result. We resent dependence because we are not in control and can be used or manipulated. We also recognize that independence is unrealistic because others often have something we need.

Conflict, therefore, occurs only between interdependent parties. We would not be in conflict with someone unless we needed something from that person. But interdependence does not mean that we must lose ourselves in order to get what we want. Interdependence requires that we bring out the value of *we*. If I am independent, I can achieve a great deal because I am self-reliant and capable. But when we work together, we can achieve much more than I could produce alone. Interdependence requires that we create a better outcome by exchanging or creating something of value to each of us.

Parties in conflict are likely to function most effectively when they are *positively goals-interdependent*. In other words, if people choose to work together to achieve their desired outcomes, they will be more inclined to coordinate their efforts, attend to one another, and have increased levels of productivity (Deutsch, 1949; Thomas, 1957). Individuals who are positively goals-interdependent also tend to like one another more and participate in more constructive communication and exchange.

This interdependent exchange is easy to grasp when the conflict is *bilateral*. A bilateral conflict is a situation in which each person wants something from the other. For example, a customer refuses to pay a supplier for an order of 100 units because the order is 10 units incomplete. The customer wants the 10 additional units, and the supplier wants payment. If neither agrees to the other's demands, there is conflict on both sides. The exchange can be more challenging, however, when the conflict is *unilateral*. A unilateral conflict is a situation in which only one party has a complaint. If a customer refuses to pay for no legitimate reason, for example, the supplier can be said to be in a unilateral conflict.

Realistically, though, would a customer refuse to pay for no legitimate reason? If the customer has the money to pay and the supplier has delivered the required number of units, withholding payment would appear to be a hostile act. Hostility originates somewhere. The customer has a reason, but either has not yet articulated it or may not be aware of it.

If we were to explore this example more closely, we might discover that earlier in the month, the customer had asked a question about product specifications. It was a busy time for the supplier, and the salesperson did not return the telephone call as quickly as in the past. When they finally made contact, the salesperson provided a brief response and indicated that the issue was "no big deal." The customer was irritated at the time, but did not press the issue any further. However, the incident stayed in the customer's unconscious throughout the month and, when it was time to pay, surfaced in the form of late payment. Did the customer make the connection between the incident and the late payment? Probably not, yet the incident acted as the catalyst for the conflict.

Unilateral conflict, therefore, is always bilateral conflict in disguise. Every conflict has its underlying causes. Sometimes the causes are conscious, and sometimes they are unconscious and buried in a cloud of seemingly unimportant and unconnected events. Therefore, a conflict may appear to be unilateral, but successful resolution still requires an interdependent, bilateral exchange. The party with the complaint must break the destructive cycle of conflict unilaterally by choosing not to react destructively. Instead, she or he must identify a need that will invite the indifferent party to participate in the exchange.

Perceived Incompatibility

The communication skills required for an interdependent, bilateral exchange can sometimes be difficult and tricky because during the course of a conflict, there is a variety of information thrown about that must be interpreted. What seems to be a simple process of two people speaking words to one another becomes much more complex when we factor in nonverbals such as gestures, facial expressions, rate of speech, or tone of voice (Figure 1-1). It becomes even more challenging when we include individual needs and drives, the history of the relationship, and external factors, such as the time of day or mental interference. Each party must interpret the information received during the course of the conflict in order to understand what is required for resolution. It is actually quite amazing that we communicate as well as we do!

The final element of the definition of conflict, *perceived incompatibility*, suggests that the complexity of the communication process interferes with each party's ability to interpret the goals and objectives of the other. Perceived incompatibility implies that many factors, most significantly our own biases, establish obstacles that make even obvious common ground and agreement difficult to establish.

Figure 1-1.   The communication process.

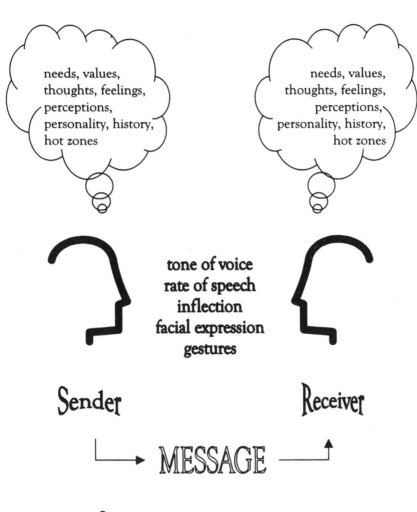

There is significant evidence that people tend to interpret behaviors, events, and outcomes in ways that support more positive definitions of themselves. For example, people will usually take credit for success and deny responsibility for failure (Ross & Sicoly, 1979). If they perform well, they will talk about how hard they worked or their superior abilities, but if they perform poorly, they point to external factors that prevented them from using their skills. People also are more likely to credit positive personality traits to themselves and to the various groups to which they belong, while assigning negative traits to other individuals and groups (Brown, 1990; Conway and Ross, 1984).

These self-serving evaluations are generally attributed to people's need for personal control and for a positive self-image. We generally pay more attention to other people's negative behaviors than to their positive behaviors because this supports the perception we have of ourselves. In other words, if I notice that someone is "better looking, smarter, and more successful" than I am, I am prone to feel like an "unattractive, stupid failure." Since I do not want to feel bad about myself, I shift my focus to the other person's negative traits. I start to find that person's faults and shortcomings. As I identify an increasing number of negative traits, the competitive balance between the other person's identity and my self-identity is restored.

This tendency is also evident in settings of group conflict. In one study, students negotiated, via written statements, a settlement in a union-management dispute over wage rates. Each party in the role-play received an identical five-page case description that contained both qualitative and quantitative information about the situation surrounding the negotiation. Before negotiating, however, the subjects were asked to provide an opinion of a fair wage rate as if they were a neutral and objective third party. The study revealed that the groups defined "fair" in ways that benefited themselves, with the students representing the union identifying higher wage rates than the students representing management. The researchers also found evidence that these self-serving assessments of fairness produced more protracted negotiations. Each party was likely to be tougher and more inflexible with an opponent who was perceived as "unfair" (Thompson and Loewenstein, 1992).

In another study, researchers asked professional negotiators to write down behaviors and tactics that they themselves or their opponents used in disputes. The subjects consistently evaluated themselves more favorably than they evaluated their negotiation opponents. They saw themselves as constructive, collaborating, better listeners, and more fair. They saw their opponents as vague, competitive, unprepared, and controlling. They also saw themselves as overall better negotiators than their opponents (De Dreu et al., 1995).

Not surprisingly, self-serving evaluations of conflict behaviors have been found to be associated with increased frustration and irritation, with reduced efforts to engage in problem solving, and with enhanced likelihood of future conflict. A self-serving perception prevents each party from being the first to cooperate. With both parties digging in their heels, it is more likely that the conflict will escalate. As conflict escalates, so do destructive behaviors, and one party's destructive behaviors are likely to provoke hostile attitudes in the other party. This, in turn, creates a downward cycle of destructive conflict behavior (Rubin et al., 1994).

Therefore, much like competition, perceived incompatibility is inherent in conflict and prevents two parties that depend on each other from finding points of agreement and resolution. But changing our perceptions is not necessarily the remedy to conflict. In fact, constructive conflict resolution does not ignore or seek to change perceptions. Constructive conflict resolution recognizes that each party's perceptions and objectives have validity and must be included as part of a total solution that includes the perceptions and objectives of all.

Factors Affecting Conflict

Before we attempt to develop strategies to identify solutions to conflict, we need to understand the variables that can influence the resolution process. These different factors demonstrate the complexity inherent in conflict and play an important role in determining whether conflict becomes constructive or destructive. When we understand the forces that can influence the intensity of a dispute, we are in a better position to manage the resolution process effectively. The factors that affect conflict include:

- The nature of the issue
- The size of the conflict
- Issue rigidity
- The situation and the environment
- Individual personalities, traits, and dispositions
- Conflict management orientation and strategies
- Cultural influences
- Conflict management skills

Nature of the Issue

Conflicts begin for a variety of reasons. While the exact origins may be difficult to trace, every conflict has issues that need to be discussed in order for the parties to reach resolution. Usually every conflict has one major issue and several minor issues. Some issues are simple, such as who should wash the dishes. Other issues are more subtle and complex, and may escalate the intensity of the interaction. For example, conflicts that revolve around having power, control, or higher status often raise the competitive stakes and lead to win-lose outcomes. Under these scenarios, constructive conflict resolution is more challenging.

It also is important to distinguish between conflicts that are based on objective issues and conflicts that are based on personal issues. An *objective* issue arises out of a particular situation and is grounded in data, facts, or conditions. Objective issues also often relate to the distribution of resources or tangible items or to rules, policies, and procedures. *Personal* issues involve specific individuals and are based on perceptions or distinct feelings about those individuals. They also often relate to values, beliefs, and the nature of the relationship. Of course, any conflict may have elements of both an objective and a personal conflict, as the following scenario illustrates.

Randi Sherman pulled her car into the driveway, happy to be home. It had been an exhausting and stressful day at her job as a sales representative for a food broker. Her day was not over, though, because she still had to work on her project for the United Way committee she was chairing. It was a good thing her husband, Steve, had agreed to cook dinner and help with the kids, she thought.

Steve was already home, and as Randi walked into the family room, he was sitting on the sofa flipping through the television channels. And, she noted resentfully, he was apparently oblivious to the messy condition of the room. It also did not look as if dinner had been started.

"Honey, what's going on here?" Randi asked.

"Boy, I'm tired tonight. I had one heck of a day!" Steve replied.

"You're tired! I've been going since six this morning, and I still have to work on this project tonight. I thought we agreed you'd take care of dinner and the kids. A little extra help around here would make it easier—but I guess that's asking too much."

"Maybe it is asking too much. You didn't have to take this extra project, you know. You said you would find the time, but as usual you're overextended."

"If you would ever pitch in with the kids and house, it would be a miracle. I'm overextended because I always have to do everything!"

This example demonstrates both an objective and a personal conflict. The objective conflict is about whether dinner had been made and the kids were being taken care of. Randi's perception was that Steve did not have dinner prepared and, because of the condition of the family room, was not attending to the children. We do not know, based on the available information, if dinner was prepared and in the refrigerator, or in the oven, or on the way from the local pizza delivery. We also do not know whether the kids were upstairs doing their homework and had agreed to pick up the family room as soon as they were finished. The conflict probably would have remained objective if Randi and Steve had stuck to those points.

The conflict became personal, however, when Randi and Steve began making accusations and calling names. Statements like, "what's going on here?" "I guess that's asking too much," and "as usual you're overextended," criticized and insulted. The verbal abuse corroded the conversation and escalated the conflict. As personal conflicts escalate, it becomes more difficult to return to a discussion of the objective conflict.

Objective disputes are not personal, and their resolution is based upon a bilateral exchange of information. Objective disputes become personal, however, when parties *intentionally* complain, criticize, or deceive as well as when parties *unintentionally* misperceive and miscommunicate. During international business negotiations, for example, conflict can occur because of cultural differences that do not have personal intentions. Each party may perceive the other party's representatives as insensitive or insulting because neither was aware of accepted customs or cultural norms. Thus, the objective conflict becomes a personal conflict because of unintentional miscommunication and misperception. In reality, the conflict remains objective with an additional issue to resolve: learning the customs of each country to avoid misunderstanding.

Personal issues are much more challenging to manage because they often elude detection, yet are considered highly important to ultimate resolution. They form intangible goals that are difficult to define because they may relate to unmet psychological needs or motivators.

A sales executive once explained, half in jest, that his work would be much easier if he did not have to deal with customers. Of course, he realized the problems inherent in his statement, but he expressed something we all feel at times. He continued, "The sales process is hindered when people let their emotions interfere with sound decision making. If customers would only stick to the objective issues related to whether my product fills the need of their business, everything would be much more expedient. But they often can't get past the color of my tie or whether I've bowed low enough or whether my boss has graced them with his presence. I spend more time feeding egos than doing business!"

The most powerful issues in conflict revolve around human needs. Despite our hopes to the contrary, all conflicts are clouded by these personal issues. Even more formal business and international conflicts contain these elements because we are not in conflict, or negotiating, with an "entity," we are in conflict with human beings. Humans have emotions, values, temperaments, viewpoints, and life experiences that shape their perspective and determine how they will approach conflict resolution.

In response to this human factor, however, we often try to remain dispassionate and unconcerned with the personal issues involved in a dispute. We somehow believe that this will make resolution easier. We try to stick to the task at hand and stay focused on the objective issues. We try to ignore the psychological needs and motivators and deal with the "important" rational issues of the conflict. But if we ignore others, if we do not attend to their ego or self-esteem issues, for example, it is likely that they will not want to interact with us. They will not trust that we are committed to satisfying their needs, and, as a result, the objective issues will be more challenging to manage.

Distinguishing between objective and personal issues is critical for our success because the strategies we ultimately select to deal with the conflict will depend upon the nature of the issues involved. It is important to go beyond a superficial analysis of the issues to identify the deeper, subtler, and often overlooked needs, goals, and objectives. This will give us the information we need to demonstrate understanding and keep the conflict headed toward constructive resolution.

Size of the Conflict

One of the characteristics of conflicts based largely on personal issues is that the disputes become larger and more intense emotionally. As the size increases and the conflict continues, each party focuses even more on personal issues, which escalates the conflict further. This self-perpetuating cycle is difficult to break unless the parties separate large and potentially overwhelming conflicts into smaller, more manageable units. The smaller the conflict, the easier it is to manage (Deutsch, 1973).

Almost every conflict involves multiple issues. But as those issues become intermingled, the conflict is harder to resolve, especially if small objective issues are mixed with larger personal issues. For example, consider a situation in which a manager of one race gives a poor performance evaluation to an employee of another race, who disagrees with the assessment. If the discussion stays focused on the criteria used to evaluate performance and the objective measurement of results, it is possible to resolve the dispute without escalation. But if the conversation moves into a discussion of attitude, traits, or personality, it probably will become personal and destructive. And what started as a conflict about different perceptions of job performance by two people of different races may turn into a conflict about race and racism. The shift from the smaller issue of job performance to the larger issue of a racial conflict intensifies the interaction and makes the conflict harder, if not impossible, to resolve.

The outcome each party expects to achieve is another factor that will influence the size of the conflict. Conflict size equals the expected difference in the value of the outcomes each party will receive (Figure 1-2) (Deutsch, 1994). For example, if a party perceives that she will achieve a favorable outcome for herself, she probably will see the conflict as small. Conversely, if a party perceives that he will lose the conflict, then he will see the conflict as larger. Even if one party believes that he can achieve a win-win solution, as long as the other party perceives that she might lose, the conflict will increase in magnitude. The greater the difference in perceptions of expected outcome, the harder it will be to manage toward constructive resolution.

These findings suggest that constructive conflict management requires that we attend to perceptions of conflict size and the various elements that influence those perceptions. By breaking down the dispute into individual components and by separating the objective issues from the personal issues, we gain a clear picture of the problem that allows for deeper understanding of the interests that must be satisfied.

Figure 1-2. Conflict size formula.

$$\text{Conflict Size} = \text{Perceived Outcome Value of Party A} - \text{Perceived Outcome Value of Party B}$$

Issue Rigidity

Whether the dispute involves a contract, a family quarrel, or a peace settlement among nations, people routinely engage in *positional conflict*. Each side takes a position, argues for it, and makes concessions to reach agreement, or at least a temporary end to the dispute. When people argue over positions, they tend to lock themselves into those positions and to use persuasion, power, aggression, or other competitive tactics to achieve their "win." The more one party tries to convince the other side to change its position, however, the more difficult it becomes to do so. Egos become invested in those positions, the competition increases, and the parties are less likely to reach agreement.

This positional approach to conflict resolution is the result of *issue rigidity*. Issue rigidity occurs when the parties perceive that there is a lack of satisfactory options or alternatives for resolving the conflict (Deutsch, 1994). Often issue rigidity is the result of perceptions of incompatibility or scarce resources. On other occasions, there may be real limits that force the parties to compete to obtain their "fair share."

The more attention that is paid to positions, however, the less attention is dedicated to identifying the underlying interests and concerns of the parties. Agreement becomes less likely and may reflect a compromise between final positions rather than a solution that is carefully crafted to meet the legitimate needs of both parties. Resolution, while obtained, is less satisfactory to each side and is likely to break down over the long term.

Consider the classic story of two sisters arguing over an orange. Each sister insisted that she was entitled to the orange. After they finally agreed to divide the orange in half, the first sister took her half, ate the fruit and threw away the rind. The other sister took her half, threw away the fruit, and used the rind in a recipe she was making. Had the sisters understood their underlying needs, they would have discovered the obvious solution: giving one the whole fruit and the other the whole rind. Their issue rigidity—needing the whole orange—prevented them from identifying the underlying needs of "satisfying an appetite" and "providing flavor."

Had those needs been identified, a variety of options for

resolution could be created. The sister who was hungry not only could enjoy the fruit, but also could eat an apple, some cookies, or, better yet, the sandwich the other sister would make for her (satisfying an additional "ego" need). The sister who needed flavor could use not only the orange rind, but also the orange spice in the spice rack, the orange-flavored liquid in the cupboard, or the lemons in the refrigerator. Once the two sisters get beyond their issue rigidity, a variety of acceptable solutions can be created.

Issue rigidity occurs when we base conflict resolution on our position or demands rather than identifying problems. Demands usually offer only one solution to a problem. But when we shift the conflict-resolution process to identifying interests and needs—or understanding the problem—we are able to recognize many solutions that can provide constructive resolution.

Situation and Environment

Conflict can be significantly affected by influences that are not directly related to the circumstances of the given dispute. Power differences, for example, influence the proceedings whenever one party has greater control or is perceived to have greater control in a conflict situation. We handle a conflict with our boss differently from the way we handle a conflict with a subordinate. We may choose to give in to our boss because we do not want to be fired, even if it is not the optimal solution for either of us. On the other hand, if we have similar issues with a subordinate, we may be more demanding, since we have direct authority over that person. In each case, the extraneous and unrelated variable of "power" influenced the resolution process.

The history of the relationship also complicates resolution because of the prior attitudes and beliefs each party may have toward the other. Previous experience creates a bias that may not be relevant to the present situation, but may be difficult to ignore. So although a party might be acting with good intentions in a current conflict, a history of past deceitfulness will influence the strategies the other party may use to resolve the present situation.

Another situational factor that influences our approach to conflict is the social environment. The way we behave in a work conflict may differ from the way we behave in a personal conflict because the social setting dictates a different set of behavioral norms. For example, it might be reasonably acceptable to "get nose-to-nose" and "talk trash" in a conflict during a pickup basketball game. However, if we used the same tactic at work in a conflict with a colleague, security would probably walk us out of the building. A conflict at work that, in reality, is as intense as a conflict on the basketball court may not even be discussed because the general climate of the office inhibits the conversation.

Finally, although it is convenient to discuss conflict in terms of two parties, many conflicts involve more than two parties. These interested third parties may influence the interactions from afar by compelling the parties into further confrontation or by encouraging them to walk away. Outsiders also often pressure the disputants into posturing simply to impress or save face with the external influence. For example, management-union negotiations tend to escalate unnecessarily as each side tries to manage both the perception of the parties inside the conflict and the perceptions of their respective constituencies.

Individual Personalities, Traits, and Dispositions

The factors within individuals that determine their personality and disposition also play an important role in determining the nature of a given conflict. People are different from one another in fundamental ways. They have different motivations, drives, values, and needs, and distinct ways of thinking, conceptualizing, perceiving, and understanding. Individuals also have unique interpersonal styles and contrasting mechanisms for coping with personal and social pressures.

These differences are easy to observe, yet we find them confounding because they pose a significant challenge to managing interactions. Often we want to change those variations in others that we see as flaws or problems; we want others to be more like us. Any of us who has tried to change another person—asked that person to think and act differently—knows the hopelessness of this task. However, in our approach to conflict, we frequently try to do just that. We attempt to persuade, cajole, and manipulate the other person into thinking like us. Sometimes we are successful, but usually the endeavor increaces the other's recictance to influence, and thus the intensity of the dispute (Brehm, 1966).

Social scientists have long been interested in the relationship between personality type and conflict management skills and outcomes. Studies have examined such variables as propensity for risk taking, need for control, tolerance for ambiguity, cognitive skills, and level of self-esteem. They also have considered individuals' need for achievement, power, and affiliation as well as their level of interpersonal trust, authoritarianism, and cooperativeness. The findings have been largely inconclusive as to whether one type is better suited for successful conflict resolution than others.

Current theories suggest, however, that all personalities interact with the structural variables in conflict in ways that shape the overall interaction. In other words, while individual differences may predispose parties to particular behavior, the nature of the issues, the traits of the other party, and pressures from third parties, among other variables, may influence and shape the actual behavior exhibited (Hamner, 1980). What seems important to constructive conflict is that the individuals have developed self-mastery and learned to choose their behavioral reactions to external stimuli. If individuals do not demonstrate an ability to monitor and regulate their behavioral reactions, then the variables of conflict may push them to act destructively. So, for example, if I am naturally inclined to be domineering and the conflict becomes overwhelming, I may choose not to remain cooperative. Instead, I may react by trying to dominate the other party, thus risk pushing the other party to react in kind with her own domineering strategy.

It does not appear that any single personality type is directly linked to successful conflict resolution. It does appear, however, that personality plays a role in the resolution process and outcome. Personality contributes to the internal needs of the conflicting parties and creates personal issues that must be managed and resolved. Constructive conflict resolution requires awareness of these differences and flexible strategies to monitor and control our own behavior.

Conflict-Management Orientation and Strategies

The interdependence of people's goals forms the basis for much of our social interaction. When people perceive their goals to be aligned, there is trust among the parties and consequently successful efforts at exchanging information and influencing one another. In contrast, when people perceive their goals to be incompatible, there is increased mistrust, and coercive power and force are used to exert influence and block the other party's efforts to attain their goals.

This represents the *dual-concerns* model of motivational orientation to conflict (Figure 1-3). One dimension describes an individual's degree of concern for obtaining his or her own outcomes, and the other dimension describes the individual's degree of concern for the other party's outcomes. Thus, the dual concerns, "concern for self" and "concern for other," are considered to be independent, and each can range from low to high. The resulting matrix provides four motivational orientations that make up the fundamental model for understanding the approaches that individuals may take during conflict.

Figure 1-3.   The dual-concerns model.

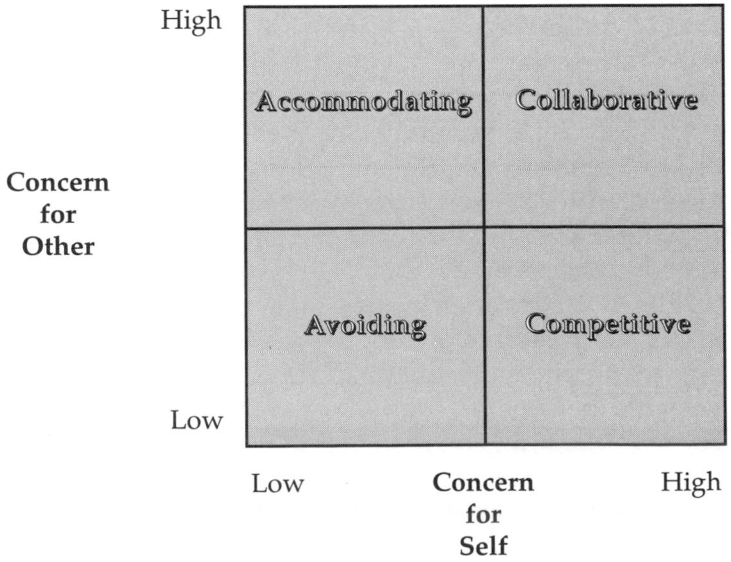

Collaborative conflict behavior is associated with high concern for self and high concern for other, and *accommodating* conflict behavior is associated with low concern for self and high concern for other. *Competitive* behavior is associated with high concern for self and low concern for other, while *avoiding* behavior is associated with low concern for self and low concern for other.

These motivational orientations shape the approach we will take to resolve a conflict. They also determine our perception of the other party and the intensity of the interaction. The more important the outcome of a given conflict is to us, the more likely we are to assume a style that will lead to achieving that outcome. The stronger the concern, the more we will try to either obtain the outcome on our own through competitive or individualistic behavior or collaborate with others to obtain the desired result. Conversely, when an issue is not important to us, we will probably choose to accommodate or avoid the conflict. When either party accommodates or avoids, there is very little concern for self and thus little if any conflict because the other party "gets his or her way." Therefore, the two orientations in the dual-concerns model that require significant interaction are collaboration and competition.

A collaborative orientation exists when the party has a positive interest in the welfare of the other as well as its own. A competitive orientation exists when the party has an interest in doing better than the other as well as doing as well as it can for itself. But additional research has demonstrated that a third orientation is required in order to present a more complete model (Deutsch, 1973). An *individualistic* orientation exists when the party has an interest in doing as well as it can for itself and is unconcerned about the welfare of the other. Individualism can be thought of as self-focused competition.

Since each of two parties can have any one of the three basic orientations, nine combinations are theoretically possible when two parties are in dispute (Figure 1-4). However, these combinations create relationship dynamics that influence the stability of the combination and cause one or both parties to change their approach to the given conflict. Research suggests that only combinations demonstrated by both sides are stable. Other combinations tend to move in the direction of mutual competition if either party has a competitive orientation. In addition, an individualistically oriented pair will move toward collaboration or mutual competition depending upon the external influences on the conflict (Deutsch, 1982).

The relative instability of the combinations and the tendency toward competition make it essential to understand the conditions that induce collaboration or competition. When one party is threatening, deceptive, condescending, or critical, the other party is likely to demonstrate similar characteristics. When one party is helpful, friendly, trusting, sensitive, and interested, the other party is more likely to mirror that behavior. Therefore, a party that is interested in maintaining a constructive environment must create the conditions that will shift the motivational orientation of the other party toward collaboration, or at least minimize the impact of a competitive orientation on the resolution process.

Figure 1-4.   The nine combinations resulting from disputing parties' orientations.

Party A Orientation	*Party B Orientation*	*Combination*
Collaborative	Collaborative	Collaborative
Collaborative	Competitive	Competitive
Collaborative	Individualistic	Competitive
Competitive	Collaborative	Competitive
Competitive	Competitive	Competitive
Competitive	Individualistic	Competitive
Individualistic	Collaborative	Competitive
Individualistic	Competitive	Competitive
Individualistic	Individualistic	Collaborative/Competitive

Cultural Influences

A marketing executive in the southeastern U.S. offices of an international telecommunications firms related a story about a conflict that she was having with a development engineer who worked in the company's San Jose, California, facility. They had clashed openly in some team meetings as well as privately in a number of telephone conversations, and the conflict was significantly affecting progress on a product development effort. The marketing executive, who was Caucasian, had recently attended a class on workplace diversity as part of an organizationwide diversity effort and was concerned that elements of her conflict with the engineer, an Asian-American male, were the result of cultural misunderstandings. After two sessions with the firm's diversity manager, she set up a meeting in San Jose to resolve the conflict. Upon her return, she reported a successful resolution, stating, "Throughout our personal challenges, I thought the cause was related to male-female or ethnic communication differences. After the first thirty minutes of our meeting, we both had a good laugh when we realized that the source of the miscommunication was that he was an engineer and I was a marketer!"

We are often in conflict with individuals or groups with different cultural backgrounds. Moreover, this diversity does not always involve obvious gender, race, or ethnic differences. It also can relate to religion, education, socioeconomic status, regions within nations, or anything else that identifies an individual as part of a larger group. As new social groups have entered the workforce and moved up in the organization hierarchy, conflicts rooted in class, gender, race, and ethnicity have become more prominent. These cultural differences create barriers to interaction, misunderstandings, prejudices, and behaviors that are unintentionally offensive and reduce the chances that conflict resolution will be constructive.

Social psychologists have long sought to identify how cultural influences affect behavior. The research has consistently concluded that we tend to like people who have attitudes and values similar to ours. This does not necessarily imply that we dislike dissimilar people. In fact, we sometimes prefer those who are different from us, but only if they have traits that are appealing or characteristics that we value. Consequently, we tend to limit most of our interdependent relationships to ethnocentric social groups.

Ethnocentrism is defined as the belief that one's own group is superior and the center of everything, with all others are evaluated with reference to it (Brewer, 1979). It is a belief that one's own group stands apart from and is better than others. Although the term *ethnocentrism* usually refers to ethnic and nationality groups, it actually applies as well to the relationship between various social categories, including income levels, profession, and educational achievement. Each social category has its own subculture, and the differences between subcultures may lead to misunderstandings, biases, and stereotypes that affect the ability of individuals in different categories to manage conflict between groups successfully.

This desire to stick to established social structures reduces the likelihood that a productive problem-solving process will occur because the self-identity of individuals is strongly linked to the characteristics of the groups with which they identify. These characteristics help to define their *social identity*. The drive toward ethnocentrism allows group members to quickly develop a sense of social identity and feel part of a desirable entity. Along with this positive sense of in-group identity goes a negative bias against those belonging to out-groups. This tendency to disparage those who are not part of one's group is unfortunately universal, whether it is applied to members of the opposite sex or to another religion, ethnicity, or nation.

Ethnocentric in-group bias occurs most consistently along philosophical or moral lines. Traits such as "trustworthiness," "honesty," and "virtue" are defined as norms that apply to members of one's own group as opposed to members of various outgroups. Cooperation within a group also rapidly builds this spirit of positive evaluation among group members, and repeated contact with members of one's own group fosters bias against members of other groups. Some researchers have found that the mere clumping of people into groups, entirely independent of any prior association or shared interest, makes them discriminate against an out-group. Moreover, the more intense the competition between groups, the greater the tendencies toward ethnocentrism in their relations (Sherif, 1966).

Muzafer and Carolyn Sherif demonstrated the impact of group cohesiveness on conflict development in a study conducted with eleven- and twelve-year-old boys at a summer camp (1966). The boys were given three days of relative freedom in which to become acquainted and establish friendships of their choosing. Then each boy was assigned to one of two groups, and their sleeping accommodations were reassigned so that the two groups were physically separated from each other. This assignment deliberately separated each boy from those with whom he had been most friendly. Initially, the new groups did not demonstrate much cohesiveness.

During the week that followed, the boys engaged in activities designed to instill cohesiveness and solidarity within each group. The boys camped out, cooked meals, improved a swimming hole, cleared athletic fields, and participated in a variety of games. Eventually, each group established its own identity and even selected a name and symbol for itself, such as Bull Dogs and Red Devils.

By the end of the week, the initial resentment had vanished and new friendships were firmly established. Most interestingly, in subsequent and very intense competitions between the two groups, the former friends turned completely against one another. In one example, the staff had arranged for a party "to let bygones be bygones." They prepared a table of refreshments, half of which were whole and delectable, and the other half crushed, soggy, and unappetizing. Unknown to the boys, the experimenters arranged for one group to arrive first; naturally, they took the most appetizing refreshments. The other group was furious when they saw what was left and called the first group names and sought revenge. The second group, for example, left the breakfast table a mess, and at lunch started a food fight. Thus, the situation set up by the researchers significantly intensified the competition as well as increased the ethnocentrism between the two groups.

Ethnocentrism can be diminished significantly with increased intergroup contact, information and education, sensitivity training, problem-solving sessions, and the use of formal procedures guiding interaction. The most significant positive changes occur when two or more groups cooperate to achieve a common goal (Sherif, 1966; Johnson & Johnson, 1989). Working toward a cooperative goal appears always to enhance other methods of reducing ethnocentrism, but without it, the other forms of interaction do not have a long-term effect. Building a common objective seems to create a perception that the out-group members share similar beliefs and values with in-group members. This perception tends to reduce the deeply personal issues that ignite a destructive conflict, and the decreased tension allows both groups to focus on objective problem resolution.

Conflict-Management Skills

Many destructive conflicts between individuals and groups result from the varying conflict-management skills possessed by the disputants. Constructive conflict management skills promote the use of cooperative strategies for handling conflict. When these competencies are not present in at least one of the parties, conflicts are more likely to become competitive, personal, and destructive. The skills can be broken down into four primary categories (Deutsch, 1994).

The first set of skills are those related to the ability to *establish an effective working relationship* with the other parties in the conflict. Each participant must be able to establish trust with the other parties and open the communication channels so that information can flow freely. An effective working relationship also allows each participant to make and respond to suggestions regarding the problem-solving process. This capability allows the parties to establish rules for conducting a negotiation that maintain a constructive environment.

The second set of skills are those related to establishing a *cooperative problem-solving attitude* toward the conflict among the conflicting parties. Humans are creatures of strong emotions with varying perceptions of the world and different styles of communicating. These factors often become intermingled with the objective aspects of the conflict. Participants must be able to separate the people from the problem in order to resolve the conflict without trying to "resolve" the people. This also requires an ability to identify, understand, and satisfy the underlying interests instead of a focus on positional bargaining. Bargaining produces quick fixes that address symptoms and does not resolve the underlying problems.

Individuals also must have skills to *manage group processes and group decision making*. Decision making in the presence of an adversary limits creativity and vision, as does insistence on "one right solution." This skill set helps clarify the nature of the problems that the conflicting parties are confronting. It also helps both parties to expand the range of alternatives that are available by facilitating creativity combined with a realistic assessment of the feasibility and desirability of the identified solutions.

None of the first three skill sets will be effective without considerable *knowledge of the issues* of the conflict. Comprehensive knowledge enables the parties to see possible solutions that might not be readily apparent. It also permits them to assess proposed solutions more realistically.

Developing conflict-management skills is critical to maintaining constructive conflict environments in both personal and group relationships. Research into the development of conflict-management skills has demonstrated the importance of this. In a variety of studies, students who were exposed to conflict-resolution training experienced more than just improvement in their ability to manage conflict. They experienced an increase in social skills and social support along with a feeling of greater empowerment. The studies also demonstrated a strong causal linkage between the training, increased self-esteem and academic performance, and decreased anxiety and depression.

Conclusions

In order to manage conflict constructively, we must increase our understanding of the factors that affect interaction and develop the tools required to establish a productive environment. But knowledge alone is not enough to make us proficient in constructive conflict resolution because the skills that are required are fundamentally different from other capabilities developed by our educational process.

Constructive conflict management depends significantly on our emotional awareness and social interaction skills, and less on our cognitive capabilities. A high IQ may, in fact, interfere with positive interaction because conflict is not always rational, and an analytical approach may overlook significant emotional needs. While we can break every conflict down into its structural components, isolate the variables, identify the problem, and develop systematic solutions, we are still dealing with humans. And no matter how "right" our answer may be, if we have not satisfied the other party's temperamental, peculiar, exacerbating personal issues, we have not resolved the conflict.

People in conflict often do not question whether they have communicated well or not. They assume they have done so without checking with the other party or examining their own internal feelings. In developing constructive conflict-management skills, external feedback is critically important. Developing conflict-resolution skills requires learning how to elicit clear feedback from others and give such feedback in return. In other words, it requires learning how to listen and inform.

The remainder of this book will attempt to increase your awareness of the strategies and tools required for constructive conflict resolution. It also will try to provide examples of good performance that you can use to compare with your own experience. None of us are beginners when we start to learn conflict-resolution skills. We all have developed strategies that may or may not be effective, and we have begun to compile mental data about our success rate. Before you can improve your skills, you must become aware of your preexisting orientations and the obstacles they may present. You must become self-aware. You also must be motivated to change any ineffective strategies. Improvement requires honest self-assessment, practice, and the courage to ask others for feedback along the way.

2

Listening to Ourselves

He who knows others is clever;
He who knows himself has discernment.
He who overcomes others has force;
He who overcomes himself is strong.

Lao Tzu, *Tao Te Ching*

The behavioral scientist Erich Fromm observed, "Hatred against oneself is inseparable from hatred against others." There is a close connection between our sense of self and the feelings we have about others (Fromm, 1939). Often we see conflicts as someone else's fault or the fault of the circumstances. The reality is, however, that disputes are frequently a reflection of the conflicts that are going on inside of us. Conflict, then, is a mirror of our own lives and attitudes.

Before we can hope to resolve external conflict with family, friends, coworkers, and others, we need to understand ourselves. In other words, before we learn to how to understand the other person and manage the external conflict in our lives, we first must learn what motivates *us* to be in conflict.

However, self-knowledge often comes with a price that creates additional internal conflict. Some of the information we receive about ourselves may be negative and may make us feel uncomfortable. We may choose not to listen to it or accept it because we are afraid of discovering that we are somehow inadequate or inferior. We may resist self-knowledge to protect our self-esteem and self-respect.

Abraham Maslow pointed out, however, that resisting personal improvement results in a "denying of our best side, of our talents, of our finest impulses, of our highest potentialities, of our creativeness. In brief, this is the struggle against our own greatness" (Maslow, 1962). Gaining self-knowledge, therefore, requires that we accept what we learn as neutral information, neither positive nor negative, that will enhance the strong capabilities that we already possess. It also requires that we continue to search for more information about ourselves by discussing our insight with others and asking for feedback. Research has shown that by disclosing ourselves to others, we will increase our self-awareness, achieve higher levels of interpersonal competence, and gain more acceptance from others. To establish an effective working relationship with others, we must first establish an effective relationship with ourselves.

Developing Self-Awareness

Self-awareness can be defined as being aware of both our emotions and our thoughts about those emotions. It is the ability to know how we feel at any point in time. At first, it might seem that our motivations, thoughts, needs, and feelings are obvious. But we all can remember times when we have been so caught up in a feeling or focused on an objective that we were oblivious to our surroundings, let alone how we really felt about something. In many cases, we realized this too late to remedy the damage that was caused by our inattention. Maybe we were having a heated disagreement with a coworker, for example, when we answered the interrupting telephone with a stern and biting, "Yeah, what?!" Then, after the caller started talking, we realized that we had just bitten the head off our best customer.

Humans are reaction machines that behave unconsciously and out of habit when confronted with difficult situations. Self-awareness, however, does not require "solving" the "problem" of our reactions. Instead, it requires becoming aware of and in touch with the emotions, needs, and thoughts that create the reactions.

Once we have awareness, we can see things that we have previously overlooked. We experience an emotional "ah-ha" of understanding and perception that helps us choose whether to act reactively or consciously to the conflict in our lives.

The Rational and Emotional Minds

Humans, much like computers, are processors of information. Information comes in through our sense receptors, and we apply a mental operation to it and thus change it. We apply another mental operation and change it again. We continue the process until we have an output that is ready to be stored in memory or used to generate some behavior. We are like computers in the sense that both can take information, operate on it, and generate some appropriate response. But unlike computers, we have two different ways of processing information.

The first mode is *rational*. Operating in the part of our brain called the neocortex, it is the mode of our conscious and is thoughtful, analytical, and reflecting. Operating simultaneously, and often independently, is another mode that is impulsive and often illogical. This *emotional* mode is quicker and more powerful than the rational mind. Controlled by the amygdala, the emotional mind takes in whole chunks of information and acts immediately without thinking (Figure 2-1). It determines such primitive reactions as whether we should fight or flee.

Unfortunately, the emotional mind is often wrong. Since it is in charge of life-or-death decisions, it uses a rapid, associative process that takes elements from the information that is received, relates them to past data stored in memory, and determines the appropriate output of behavior. However, the emotional mind operates based on its *perceptions* of the data. How information seems or what it reminds us of is far more important than the reality of that information. The emotional mind associates current information with the feelings or moods of the memory and reacts to the current situation without distinguishing it from the past.

Figure 2-1. The rational and emotional minds.

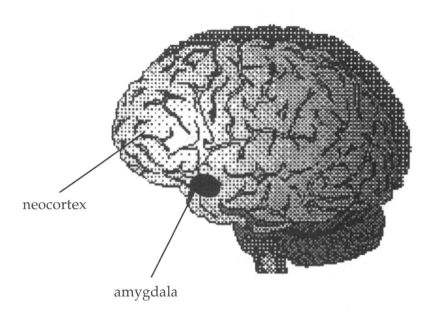

neocortex

amygdala

The rational mind, in contrast, is not as interested in associations as it is in objective information. It wants facts, figures, and data. It wants to weigh the information carefully, analyze it, contemplate it, compare it to past data, and produce logical behavioral output. But by the time the rational mind has completed its examination, the faster and more action-oriented emotional mind has generated a behavior. It may be the wrong behavior, but by then it is too late. To paraphrase the American author Ambrose Bierce, speak with the emotional mind and you will make the best speech you will ever regret.

Although they operate differently, the emotional and rational minds together help us to make sense of the varied information we receive from our external environments. The emotional mind reacts to a stimulus, and then the rational mind determines from additional feedback whether it was the appropriate reaction. The emotional mind reacts again, the rational mind weighs the logic of the reaction, and so on. For example, imagine that you are driving down the highway in your car when, all of a sudden, you see movement out of the corner of your eye. Your emotional mind receives the data and commands your heart to beat faster, your breathing rate to increase, and your foot to lift the brake. Your rational mind then determines that it was a bird flying by the car and that there are no other objects nearby that could present a danger. Your emotional mind receives this additional information and tells your heart and breathing rates to return to normal and your foot to move off the brake. Your rational mind evaluates the conditions one more time before you continue driving down the highway.

When we communicate, these two modes of processing information work in this fashion to make sense of the verbal and nonverbal information presented by the other party. The rational mind attempts to sort out the literal meaning of the information presented. The emotional mind attempts to associate the new words, tone of voice, rate of speech, and body signals with past feelings and perceptions. Even if this communication is unfamiliar information, the emotional and rational minds labor away to identify the appropriate behavioral reaction or the correct location to store the information for later use.

Frederic Bartlett was one of the first to examine this process of making sense of verbal information (Bartlett, 1932). In his research, Bartlett asked students to read a folk story from an unfamiliar culture. Then, much like a game of "telephone," he asked the students to repeat the story to the next person, and so on. By the time the story reached the last person in the line, it was completely changed. Many details and names were missing. The references to spirits and ghosts were eliminated, and new events were added so that the story would make sense in the cultural context of the students. Bartlett concluded that humans do not passively record verbal information and randomly forget some of it. Rather, humans make an "effort after meaning." That is, they make an active attempt to make sense out of the information they receive by attempting to make it fit with what they already know and are familiar with.

Schank and Abelson proposed another way to think about this. They suggested that humans maintain specialized scripts for recurring episodes of their experience and that we use these scripts for comprehending verbal information (Schank and Abelson, 1977). When someone tells you something in a conversation, you search your memory to try to find the appropriate script. Your mind tries to determine whether the information fits the restaurant script, the take-the-plane script, the buying-groceries script, and so on. Once you determine which script is appropriate, comprehending what is being said becomes easier.

But the communication we receive does not always fit our standardized scripts from memory. We might have to use a modified script in order to make sense of the information. For example, if someone was telling us about going out to dinner, we might immediately think of our restaurant script for "Chez Magnifique." In that script, we are seated by a host and given menus. The waiter unfolds our cloth napkins, we order wine from a wine steward, and we eat an exquisite meal prepared by a talented chef. Instead, the storyteller describes standing in line to order food, finding his own table, and cleaning up before he left the restaurant. It takes our rational mind a while to determine that we need to use the cafeteria or fast-food restaurant script. In the meantime, our emotional mind has us feeling confused or agitated, and sends these signals first to our rational mind and then to the storyteller as nonverbal, behavior signals.

The emotional mind can create significant confusion in our rational mind. Emotions tend to lie just beneath the surface of awareness, but are the guiding force behind our actions and decisions. Decisions such as whether to get married, which car to buy, what to wear, or even which entrée to choose on the never-ending Chinese restaurant menu are influenced by strong feelings that are not necessarily registering in our rational mind. The resulting confusion often causes us to freeze with indecisiveness, unable to make a logical choice. But as we know, logic seems to have less to do with these decisions than does emotion. Our rational mind ultimately seems to decide by factoring in our intuition and how we "feel" about the choices.

But what happens when our rational mind refuses to listen to our emotional mind? How is our behavior influenced when we ignore our feelings and intuition? Or how do we deal with the variety of often confusing signals that are sent to our rational mind?

Repression and Resistance

Tom managed a department of five chemists for an international pharmaceutical company. He considered himself a man of strong religious convictions, and although he never "preached" at work, his principles created a moral code of conduct that governed his thoughts, decisions, and behavior. Tom believed in treating people fairly and with kindness.

One of Tom's employees, Michael, was considered by many in the industry to be a brilliant chemist. Michael had graduated with honors from a top university and, in addition to being published, had received a prestigious scholarly award. In the seven years he had worked for the company, he had proved to be an outstanding employee. He was well liked among his coworkers as well as by those in other departments, and was considered a good team player. Michael often chose to take on extra projects that others found too challenging and never failed to deliver results that met or exceeded expectations. Although it was never discussed openly or made "official," Michael was a gay man.

Despite Michael's solid qualifications and performance, Tom refused to promote him or give him the positive recommendation needed for an internal transfer, although he promoted others who were considered to be less qualified. When Michael asked for feedback, Tom provided a litany of "objective" criticisms. He stated that Michael was sound technically, but lacked the necessary characteristics and qualifications to climb the management ladder. He identified small oversights in Michael's work product and deficiencies in his administrative capabilities. This disagreement caused significant tension in the department. Eventually, Tom was promoted to another position. During the eighteen months after Tom's departure, Michael received two promotions.

When questioned by a human resources manager, Tom reaffirmed his reasons for not promoting Michael. And when an organization psychologist later interviewed Tom about this situation, she concluded that, while Tom seemed to suspect Michael's sexual orientation, he did not state that he knew for sure. She also reported that Tom was resolutely convinced that his decision not to promote Michael was rational and correct, although Michael's performance evaluations, experience, and education did not support this conclusion.

Quite possibly, Tom's unconscious feelings about Michael's sexual orientation influenced his decision. Tom could not reconcile subconsciously the principle of treating people fairly and with kindness with his moral conviction that homosexuality was wrong. Consequently, his emotional mind sent confusing messages to his rational mind. Not wanting to deal with this confusion, the rational mind selectively interpreted the emotional information and perceived faults that would support his conclusions.

When we refuse to acknowledge information coming from our emotional mind, we are *repressing* that information. When people repress certain thoughts, feelings, or memories, they do so because they regard them as threatening in some way. The feelings or memories will be repressed if we consider them wrong, inappropriate, immoral, unrealistic, or irrational. We move them so far into our subconscious that we are often unaware of their existence, and we ignore the messages they send to the rational mind.

Repression is a defense. The unacceptable wish and various thoughts associated with it are pushed out of consciousness to ward off undesired emotional and, in many cases, physical pain. Research conducted by Daniel Weinberger, a psychologist who pioneered the study of repression, demonstrated that while some people may seem cool, calm, and collected outwardly, they often are overwhelmed with physical and psychological confusion that they do not notice. In one study conducted by Weinberger, volunteers were administered sentence-completion tests and monitored for their level of physiological arousal. When presented with sentences about violent or disturbing situations, the volunteers identified as repressors showed physical signs of anxiety such as increased heart rate and sweating and higher blood pressure. When asked about their emotional state, however, they said they felt normal (Weinberger, 1990).

Weinberger has found that one out of every six people can be considered a repressor and demonstrates an ongoing and consistent pattern of tuning out emotions such as anger, fear, hurt, or anxiety. But to some extent, we all occasionally use this strategy to protect ourselves from emotional confusion and discomfort. Repression builds a wall around certain acts, impulses, thoughts, or memories that we do not want to escape from our unconscious.

Unless we are repressors, however, emotions usually evade our attempts to repress them and sneak into a more conscious level of our awareness. But since they are still uncomfortable, we use a strategy called *resistance* to avoid a head-on confrontation with these emotions. An individual who is practicing resistance may, for example, show more significant signs of being physically uncomfortable when discussing certain subjects. He may fidget in his chair, tap his foot, or change his rate of breathing. Eventually, he might try to change the subject, break off a train of thought, or say, "Whatever," and move to the next topic. Resistance, as Freud concluded, is the overt manifestation of some powerful force that opposes the recovery of critical memories into consciousness (Freud, 1917). The memories are more conscious than in the case of repression, but they still are not dealt with directly.

Repression and resistance appear to be successful strategies for regulating our emotions, but they may be costly to our self-awareness and our ability to manage conflict. On the one hand, we are able to insulate ourselves from emotional pain and confusion that prevent our rational mind from operating effectively. On the other hand, our rational mind does not receive important information that may improve our understanding of the issues of the conflict and help us make better overall decisions.

Conflict, even at its most constructive, causes our emotional mind to work overtime. The current dispute may feel familiar or remind us of other similar disputes in the past. It may generate strong positive or negative emotions that interfere with our ability to make sense of the communication from the other party. When we repress or resist thoughts, feelings, or memories, we may misunderstand what is said and react in a way that fans the flames of the disagreement.

Identifying the source of our repression and resistance may be challenging, take years of psychotherapy and counseling, and still not help us resolve conflict. However, *awareness* of our emotional state or condition can open pathways to comprehension and constructive conflict resolution. In other words, you can be sure that if you are involved in a conflict with someone, you need to look inside yourself to identify ignored or resisted feelings, moods, and thoughts. You must become aware of the emotions that contribute either consciously or unconsciously to continued disagreement.

Identifying Your Interpersonal Zones

Part of self-awareness then, is identifying what we are feeling. The problem with this is that very often we are simply not aware of repressed or resisted emotions. If we are not aware of these emotions, how can we be expected to identify them? Furthermore, if we identify these emotions, they may have such a dramatic impact on our self-concept and self-esteem that we become extremely defensive and more resistant to additional self-awareness.

An easier place to start to develop self-awareness is to identify our core interpersonal zones. Interpersonal zones can be broken into two categories, or levels, of awareness (Figure 2-2). The first category, composed of comfort zones and hot zones, relates to an outer zone of self-awareness where we are more conscious of the emotional underpinnings of our behavior. The second category, made up of value zones, social zones, and cognitive zones, is associated with an inner zone of deeper, more unconscious preferences that shape our actions.

As we develop awareness of our interpersonal zones, we begin to understand our strengths and our vulnerabilities. We discover what we value, how we interact, and how we form impressions of the world. Most importantly, we begin to see quite plainly how these interpersonal zones help and hinder constructive conflict management.

Figure 2-2. Interpersonal zones and levels of awareness.

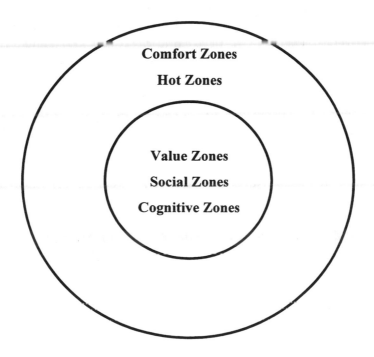

Comfort Zones and Hot Zones

A *comfort zone* represents a range of emotions and behavior where we are at our best. Comfort zones are the situations in which we are truly calm, cool, and collected, and in which we achieve our peak performance. In conflict, we are in our comfort zone when interaction seems easy and natural, the dispute remains constructive, we exchange information freely, and we achieve outcomes that are satisfactory to both parties.

We are out of our comfort zone when the interaction or communication does not go as smoothly. We may begin to feel more agitated, frustrated, or upset, and want to blame the other party for the breakdown in communication. We become defensive or protective, or we feel that we want to go on the attack. In these situations, we are probably out of our comfort zone because the other party has triggered a hot zone.

A *hot zone* is an area of personal vulnerability that generates an intense emotional reaction to a specific situation, event, or person. Hot zones can be external events that trigger a behavioral reaction, or they can be mental or behavioral blocks that prevent us from overcoming obstacles to successful interaction. Hot zones exist in the emotional mind and are caused by unconsciously associating the current situation with a negative memory. They exist because of our perception of the present, not necessarily because of the current reality. The association generates emotions that challenge our self-concept or exert pressure to change our thoughts or behavior. Most often, however, we slide back into our established, but ineffective, patterns of behavior and fall victim to our vulnerability.

According to legend, Achilles, the hero of Homer's *Iliad* and the son of the sea goddess Thetis, was plunged by his mother into the river Styx to render him invulnerable. The deed was successful except that the heel by which she held him remained untouched by the water. The one weak spot, his heel, was both a symbol of his mortality and his eventual downfall. He knew of his weak spot, and others warned him against doing battle. Rather than accepting his vulnerability and safeguarding against it, he sought to prove his invincibility by going off to fight the Trojan War. While he won many heroic battles, he was eventually slain by an opponent, Paris, who wounded him in his vulnerable heel with a poisoned arrow.

Like Achilles, we each have at least one weak spot or vulnerability that regularly trips us up. Hot zones can be internal, often unconscious choices that relate more directly to our overall self-concept. They are weaknesses or preferences that we let define our self-worth. Achilles had only a few inches of weakness, but those few inches determined his fate. When we let our insecurities convince us that those "few inches" are more important than the rest of our capabilities, we face a losing battle with ourselves. We spend more time in trying to make up for our shortcomings than in improving upon our already solid foundation.

Consider the case of Sandra, a manager in the telemarketing department of a financial services firm. Sandra was new to her position and wanted her employees to like her. She hoped that if they respected and appreciated her, they would be more willing to help her achieve the high expectations she had for the department. So, rather than express her anger at minor irritations with her employees, she bit her tongue, trying instead to focus on bigger concerns. Nevertheless, the irritations piled up until she could no longer control herself and she would, as her employees complained, "explode like a volcano" with rage. Sandra shifted between no contact with employees and furious contact to the point that her employees feared her. Their fear, in turn, increased the number of errors in their work, which increased the frequency of her explosions, and so on.

Sandra's hot zone, not knowing how to express minor criticisms, actually created an environment that increased the number of incidents to criticize. The result was an increase in conflict with her employees. She found that when she tried to ignore or suppress her hot zone, it reappeared when she least desired it. The more she focused on her shortcoming, the less control she had over it. Soon she, and consequently others, defined herself as an explosive personality. Gone was the excited new manager with solid capabilities and great ideas for improvement.

What we resist persists. Sandra's problem was not strong emotions generated by minor displeasure, but rather her attitude toward them. By seeing criticism as negative, she underestimated her ability to help improve employee performance. Instead of learning from her vulnerability and changing her behavior, she let it become the guiding force behind her interaction with others. In other words, as long as we see our hot zone as a defect, it will continue to plague us. However, when we recognize that it represents only a "few inches" of our total package, we are better able to support our own efforts at self-improvement.

One useful technique for becoming more aware of our hot zones is to give them nicknames. Sandra found this technique quite effective. When she admitted that she exploded by "ranting, throwing temper tantrums, and kicking the dirt at her feet," she said she must seem like the cartoon character Yosemite Sam. From that point on, whenever she or her employees saw that she was feeling agitated, they would say, "Here comes Yosemite," and all begin to laugh. The emotional relief allowed Sandra to make her point more effectively and allowed her employees to be more accepting of her direction.

When situations become too uncomfortable, we protect ourselves so that our self-concepts can remain intact. As soon as we find ourselves outside our comfort zones, we react, defend, attack, rationalize, or make excuses that guide us back to the safety of our standard self-concept and behavior. Not only do we avoid confrontation with repressed emotions, we also resist self-improvement that would be otherwise beneficial. We see the hot zone as a problem and our comfort zone as the solution.

In reality, comfort zones and hot zones are neither good nor bad. They are simply information that helps us maintain self-awareness during conflict. Without this self-awareness, our rational mind is not able to make sense of the confusing signals that are sent by our emotional mind. Maintaining an inventory of our comfort zones and hot zones helps us identify situations that increase the likelihood that we will engage in destructive conflict behavior. It also helps us re-create situations that lead to constructive resolutions.

The first step toward discovering your comfort zones and hot zones is to make an inventory of the situations in which you are at ease and those in which you are uncomfortable. We all have shortcomings that interfere with our ability to manage conflict and reach our full potential in our career and personal relationships. The following exercises will help you assess the conditions that influence your conflict behavior.

You may have to probe beneath the surface to identify your real hot zones. For example, for hot zone question 5, you might respond that you are your own worst enemy because you procrastinate. At first glance, procrastination is your hot zone. However, when you begin to explore *why* you procrastinate, you might discover that you are not confident of your abilities or you fear criticism or you have agreed to something you do not really want to do. One or all of those reasons may be the real hot zone.

Exercise 1: Identify Your Comfort Zones

1. Consider conflicts in your professional and personal life in which you felt at ease and in which the resolution was successful.

2. Identify the nature of the conflict and the issues involved.
3. Make a list of the behaviors you exhibited that made the conflict constructive.
4. Make a list of the behaviors other parties exhibited that made the conflict constructive.
5. Identify trends or common themes.

Exercise 2: Identify Your Hot Zones

1. Consider conflicts in your professional and personal life that were difficult or that became destructive. Also, identify situations in which you constantly complain, feel frustrated, feel helpless, become obsessed, or feel mentally exhausted.
2. Make a list of the factors that generated these intense emotions.
3. Write down your response to the other person's behavior.
4. Identify trends or common themes.
5. What do you or other people mean by the statement that you are your own worst enemy?
6. In what areas of your life would you like to achieve more? Consider your career, family, hobbies, and activities. What is holding you back?
7. What would make your career more satisfying? What is preventing you from making this change?
8. What would make your personal relationships more satisfying? What is preventing you from making this change?
9. What types of situations do you avoid? Why?
10. What is guaranteed to increase your stress level? What is guaranteed to put you in a bad mood?
11. Where would you like more recognition and attention? What are you doing about it?
12. Why are you sometimes difficult to get along with?
13. When are you likely to forgo your own wants, needs, and desires in order to please someone else?
14. What would give your life more meaning and purpose?

You should conduct this same assessment after each conflict you encounter. As soon as you can after such a situation, take an objective look at what occurred during the dispute. This ongoing analysis will help you increase your self-awareness and prepare you to manage the next conflict constructively. Remember that the most important thing is not solving the "problem." It is becoming aware of and in touch with the problem so that you can choose whether to act reactively or consciously. You also might consider discussing some of the questions with a family member, friend, or coworker. Sometimes another person's feedback is helpful in providing accurate answers.

Value Zones

Comfort zones and hot zones are areas of self-awareness that are easier to understand than others because there is a more apparent behavioral or emotional connection. We know we are in a comfort zone, for example, because we *feel* at ease and we *achieve* a higher level of performance. This outer zone of self-awareness represents the emotional and behavioral result of an inner zone of perceiving and processing information. The inner zone is composed of three additional areas that shape what we believe, or *value zones,* how we interact, or *social zones,* and how we think, or *cognitive zones.* This core to our self-concept is based on our temperament or preferences and determines *why* we each perceive, feel, and behave differently from others.

A *value zone* is the range of prioritized central attitudes that helps us define what is right or wrong. Value zones form a core for many of our beliefs, emotions, and behaviors. They also provide a frame of reference that helps it interpret incoming information to know how to make value-based decisions. While values are among our most stable and enduring characteristics, we are not always conscious of what we really value and we often behave in ways that are inconsistent with those values. For example, Kerry, a marketing executive with a consumer products company, stated that her family and personal leisure time were her two highest priorities, yet she frequently worked ten- and twelve-hour days, including weekends. In a sense, she was substituting a goal with an immediate payoff—the intrinsic and extrinsic rewards from work—for her more long-term, central values. Consequently, her frustration level increased, conflicts with her family escalated, and she was gradually less productive at work.

When we are not conscious of our value zones and act or make decisions that are outside of or inconsistent with them, we become frustrated and ineffective. Lack of awareness also can increase the intensity or destructive nature of conflict, since our values strongly influence the way we perceive incoming communication. When we understand not only what we value, but also how we prioritize our values, interaction with those who may have different priorities becomes easier to manage.

Milton Rokeach proposed that the total number of values that individuals have is relatively small and definable and that all individuals have the same values, only in different degrees (Figure 2-3) (Rokeach, 1973). In other words, we all value courtesy, but some of us make it a higher priority than others do. Rokeach also indicated that values can be separated into two distinct categories: *terminal*, or ends-oriented; and *instrumental*, or means-oriented.

A *terminal value* is an end state of existence that an individual or society wants to attain. According to Rokeach, terminal values are either personal, such as "peace of mind," or social, such as "world peace." When we increase the priority of one personal value, other personal values also increase in priority. At the same time, social values decrease in priority. Likewise, when we increase in priority of one social value, other social values increase in priority while the personal values decrease in priority. For example, if you were to increase your priority for "world peace," the priority of "equality" would also increase. At the same time, you would subconsciously decrease the priority you placed on the personal values of "happiness," "pleasure," and "social recognition."

Instrumental values are modes of conduct and interaction that we define as personally and socially preferable in all situations, and that relate to either morality or competence. Rokeach suggested that strong emotions are generated when we make decisions or act contrary to our instrumental values. For example, if we behave dishonestly, violating a moral value, we feel guilty, whereas if we lose self-control, a competence value, we feel shameful.

Two parties engaged in conflict often have different value zones. This intensifies the dispute because our basis of "right"

Figure 2-3.   Terminal and instrumental values.

Terminal Values	Instrumental Values
A comfortable life (a prosperous life)	Ambitious (hardworking, aspiring)
An exciting life (a stimulating, active life)	Broadminded (open-minded)
A sense of accomplishment (lasting contribution)	Capable (competent, effective)
A world at peace (free of war and conflict)	Cheerful (lighthearted, joyful)
A world of beauty (beauty of nature and the arts)	Clean (neat, tidy)
Equality (brotherhood, equal opportunity for all)	Courageous (standing up for your beliefs)
Family security (taking care of loved ones)	Forgiving (willing to pardon others)
Freedom (independence, free choice)	Helpful (working for the welfare of others)
Happiness (contentedness)	Honest (sincere, truthful)
Inner harmony (freedom from inner conflict)	Imaginative (daring, creative)
Mature love (sexual and spiritual intimacy)	Independent (self-reliant, self-sufficient)
National security (protection from attack)	Intellectual (intelligent, reflective)
Pleasure (an enjoyable, leisurely life)	Logical (consistent, rational)
Salvation (saved, eternal life)	Loving (affectionate, tender)
Self-respect (self-esteem)	Obedient (dutiful, respectful)
Social recognition (respect, admiration)	Polite (courteous, well-mannered)
True friendship (close companionship)	Responsible (dependable, reliable)
Wisdom (a mature understanding of life)	Self-controlled (restrained, self-disciplined)

Source: Milton Rokeach, *The Nature of Human Values* (New York: Free Press, 1973), p. 28.

and "wrong," an important component of our self-concept, is determined by the prioritization of our values. However, as mentioned in Chapter 1, our value zones are shaped by a variety of individual preferences and social cultural influences, not by a set of universal truths. Therefore, it is not necessarily a matter of right or wrong, good or bad, but rather a matter of priority differences that are relative to each ethnocentric group. When we are in conflict with someone with different values, or when we perceive a challenge to our values, this threatens our sense of self at a subconscious level. Unless we are aware of our value zones, the threat will remain at the subconscious level and we will have a harder time resolving the conflict.

Understanding how we prioritize our values is the first step toward value-zone self-awareness, but understanding how to use our values to make decisions and guide our behavior is a more sophisticated level of awareness. Lawrence Kohlberg proposes that our behavior grows out of our level of *values maturity*, or what he calls moral maturity. He suggests that, much as in any other form of human development, people progress from one level of values maturity to another, and as they do, their value priorities change. When our values come into conflict with one another, how we decide which value takes precedence—in other words, how we exercise our value judgment—may depend upon our particular stage of development (Hersh, Paolitto, Reimer, 1979).

Kohlberg's model of values maturity consists of three major levels, with each level containing two stages of development. Individuals at the *preconventional level* (stages 1 and 2 of his model) approach moral issues from the perspective of the concrete interests of the people involved. They are not concerned with what society defines as the proper way to behave, but only with the concrete consequences that the individuals would face in deciding upon a particular action. For example, "Will I get fired if I am insubordinate and disagree with my boss?" Individuals at the *conventional level* (stages 3 and 4) approach moral issues by taking into consideration the moral norms of society. They strive not only to avoid punishment, but also to live by the accepted definitions of a good member of the social group. "I should not disagree with my boss because I don't want to get fired and because, as a team player, I should support his decision." Finally, individuals at the *postconventional*, or *principled, level* (stages 5 and 6) approach moral problems by looking beyond the given norms and laws of their society to base decisions upon their own internalized principles. That is, they make judgments based on a set of abstract, autonomous principles that have been developed from personal experience. "I should determine whether to agree or disagree with my boss based on whether the data (my principles) support his decision."

Carol Gilligan later enhanced Kohlberg's notion of the postconventional level of reasoning. Her research discovered a mode in which, rather than being abstract and divorced from a particular time and place, as Kohlberg suggested, the highest level of moral reasoning focused on concrete interpersonal relationships that extended over time. She suggests that adult values maturity goes beyond independent intellectual thought, or autonomy, as its sole criterion to include interdependence, responsibility, and caring for others (Gilligan, 1977).

Both Kohlberg and Gilligan agree, however, that few individuals reach the postconventional level of values maturity. Once we reach adolescence, we have reached stage 4, and our moral reasoning has developed its full formal operations. At this stage, our level of values maturity is consistent with that of most adults. We progress to the postconventional level only when we are faced with difficult moral dilemmas to which the solutions are not defined adequately by society's norms and laws. The stress and anxiety that we feel forces a *self-confrontation* that makes us aware of the inconsistency between our values and our self-concept. We realign a central value to resolve the moral dilemma, and as a result, the less central beliefs and behaviors change.

Developing our values maturity requires that we develop a set of internalized principles that will guide our behavior. These principles, discussed more fully in Chapter 3, will help create more effective behavior and decision making during conflict. This development is enhanced the more we are aware of our value zones. Awareness of our value priorities helps provide perspective on the value zones and maturity level of others, and gives us a deeper understanding of how to manage our conflicts more constructively.

Exercise 3: Identify Your Value Zones

To help you determine your value zones, examine the lists of terminal and instrumental values presented in Figure 2-3. For each set of values, rank the items from 1 to 18 in order of preference, with 1 being most important and 18 being least important. As a first step, you may want to identify each value as being of high, moderate, or low importance. Once you have divided the values into three separate categories, it will be easier to rank them within each category.

Remember, we do not always act in accordance with our values, so you might consider what your current conflicts or hot zones may be trying to tell you about your value zones. There are no right or wrong answers, only preferences that guide our reactions. Awareness of our preferences will help us consciously decide how to react effectively when we are in conflict with others.

Social Zones

After three years managing the accounts receivable department, Donna could not wait to be transferred back to a staff-level analyst position. While she would miss the prestige and pay that came with being a "manager," she would not miss "managing." As she stated, "I thought I was pretty good with people before I started this job, but I don't ever want to get involved with employees again. When you're a manager, your people want to talk to you about *everything.* It's one problem after another, and it makes you want to pull your hair out! I want to go back into my little cubicle with my computer and calculator and be left alone to do my job."

There were only four employees in Donna's department, and their performance was consistently above average.

Other departments perceived her group as a true team, with great attitudes and a solid work ethic. When asked to illustrate the types of problems that she dealt with, Donna did not describe major personality conflicts or disagreements over work process and policy. She identified only what could be described as common work-related issues or questions asking for clarification of company policies and procedures. So, why was she so frustrated? Why did Donna feel overwhelmed with the interaction?

Much of the answer lies in another important area of self-awareness, our social zones. *Social zones* relate to our interpersonal orientation and describe our preference in regard to interaction with and our behavioral tendencies toward other people. Since managing conflict requires a significant amount of interaction with people, knowledge of our social zones helps us tap into the social zones of others and keep the conflict constructive. When we are unaware of this key interpersonal factor, we may misperceive the other party's intentions, send confusing signals, or become frustrated and dissatisfied with the interaction.

Our social zones do not necessarily describe our actual behavior patterns in social situations. Rather, they describe our preferences and tendencies to behave in certain ways regardless of the external situation. For example, you may prefer to avoid parties and instead stay home and read a book. But since your job requires that you attend social functions, you have learned to tolerate, if not succeed at, parties. Your preference is to avoid social interaction, although your behavior demonstrates otherwise. Our internal needs and motivators define our social zones, not our overt behavior or external influences.

One useful model for assessing your social zones is based on a theory about personality types developed by Swiss psychiatrist Carl Jung. Jung suggested that people draw their energy from different sources. *Extraverts* are energized from the external world of people, activities, and things, whereas *introverts* are energized from the inner world of ideas, emotions, and impressions. We are not either extraverted or introverted. Rather, we fall somewhere on a continuum with extraversion at one end and introversion at the other.

Extraverts prefer to be social because they draw their energy from the interaction. They look for stimulation outside of themselves and tend to have a wide range of interests and activities. Extraverts communicate outwardly and with excitement. They want to engage others in dialogue and like to talk through ideas. As one extravert once described, "If I don't speak my ideas as soon as they come into my head, I'm afraid I will lose them." In conflict, extraverts are more likely to share information as a strategy for resolution, even if it is personal or potentially damaging.

Introverts, in contrast, prefer solitude in order to recharge their batteries. They seem to draw their energy from meditating, reflecting, or working alone. Introverts are inclined to keep their ideas to themselves, and prefer to think carefully before acting on their thoughts. They enjoy interacting with others, but it often drains their energy or becomes overwhelming. During conflict, introverts are likely to need personal and physical space to contemplate what has been said, and at times may appear aloof from the interaction.

The differences between extraversion and introversion often lead to misunderstandings. In the earlier example, Donna, an introvert, was overwhelmed by the interaction with her employees. The conflicts she had to resolve often were not really conflicts, but became conflicts because of misperception. When Donna grew exhausted from conversation with her extraverted employees, she retreated to her office to recharge. Her employees occasionally perceived the withdrawal as a lack of concern, but most often they thought Donna was researching an answer. So, like true extraverts, they persisted and continued to follow up until they got their answer, much to Donna's dismay.

On bad days, Donna saw her employees as bothersome, not able to solve their own problems, and more interested in talking than in working. At the same time, her employees often saw Donna as distant and slow to make a decision. In reality, they each had different social zones. Different social zones require different strategies for interaction. Fortunately, while Donna managed the department, she and her employees usually gave

each other the benefit of the doubt, and the working relationships were able to remain intact. But without increased awareness of their different preferences, the long-term interaction
would probably have grown personal and destructive. Donna's
subconscious realization of this motivated her to take the non-
management position.

Another model that helps illustrate and expand the concept
of social zones is the Fundamental Interpersonal Relationship
Orientation, or FIRO, developed by Dr. Will Schutz. It suggests
that people's behavior in interpersonal relationships is based on
three different need dimensions (Schutz, 1958). The basic assumption of the model is that we all seek to establish compatible
relationships with other people. To avoid conflict in those relationships, however, three interpersonal needs must be satisfied.
The first is the need for *inclusion*. That is, we need to maintain a
relationship with other people, to be included in their activities
or to include them in our own activities. But when we factor in
extraversion and introversion, the level of inclusion may vary. In
other words, sometimes we want to be social, but other times we
want to be left alone. Therefore, our need for inclusion falls
somewhere between *expressed inclusion,* the need to include others, and *wanted inclusion,* the need to be included by others.

The primary concern of inclusion is to determine whether
we fit in. Does the group accept us? Do we accept the group?
This social comparison helps us refine our social zones by refin-
ing our definition of self. We identify what roles and boundaries
are acceptable to us.

The second interpersonal need is the need for *control*. We all
need to maintain some power and influence in our relationships.
Sometimes we want to lead and direct, but other times we want
to be led and directed. At all times, however, we want to feel as
if we have the freedom and independence to choose whether we
control or are controlled. In other words, we seek to balance *expressed control,* the need to control others, with *wanted control,* the
need to be controlled by others. The need for control helps us to
determine our level of competence and our ability to influence
others.

Finally, we also have a need for *affection,* or the need to form
close personal relationships with others. We want to feel appre-

ciated and we want to appreciate others, but at the same time, we try to maintain some social distance. Here again, our preferences for extraversion or introversion can determine our needs for *expressing affection* toward other people and for *wanting affection* from them. Our need for affection relates directly to how comfortable we are in sharing our thoughts and feelings with others. This need helps us determine whether we are personally liked as well as the level of emotion that it is acceptable to show to others.

Our needs for inclusion, control, and affection, when integrated with extraversion and introversion, provide a useful set of tools to examine our social zones. Awareness of how we balance these needs can provide important insight into our perceptions of specific conflicts. Many of our emotional reactions in conflict are caused not by objective differences, but by variations in these interpersonal preferences. Knowledge of our social zones helps us understand what we require in order to manage our emotions and keep resolution constructive.

Because conflicts take many different shapes and forms, it is important that you understand your own social zones to increase the chances of success in the resolution process. The following exercise will help you assess this aspect of your interpersonal preferences. After completing the exercise, you might consider discussing some of the questions with a family member, friend, or coworker.

Exercise 4: Identify Your Social Zone

Read the two statements in each row. Place a check next to the statement that best describes you. Total the number of checks in each column.

Column A	Column B
_____ Like to do several things at once.	_____ Like to do one thing at a time.
_____ Talk while you think.	_____ Think before you talk.
_____ Like working with other people.	_____ Like working alone.

____ Develop ideas by   ____ Develop ideas by
     discussion.   reflection.
____ Enter relationships freely ____ Enter relationships
     and meet people easily.   slowly and meet people
                                    selectively.
____ Do–Think–Do.   ____ Think–Do–Think.
____ Prefer face-to-face   ____ Prefer written
     communication.   communication.
____ Initiate conversation.   ____ Wait to be approached.
____ Tolerate crowds and noise. ____ Avoid crowds and seek
                                    quiet.
____ Like having many   ____ Like having a few close
     acquaintances and friends.   friends.
____ Total   ____ Total

Scoring: Total the number of checks in each column. The score approximates where you fall on the continuum representing Extraversion and Introversion, columns A and B, respectively. A score of 10 in one column and 0 in the other represents a strong preference for the style of interaction receiving ten checks. A score of 5 in one column and 5 in the other represents no preference for either style.

Cognitive Zones

A couple of years ago, a young professional couple I know were considering whether to build a new home. They had decided upon a house plan and contractor, and all they needed was a lot on which to build. One Saturday afternoon, as they were driving through the housing developments in their community, the husband stopped the car, jumped out, and ran onto a vacant lot across the street, shouting, "This is it!" As his wife made her way to the property, he leaped around the lot exclaiming, "Honey, can't you just see it? This feels perfect. The house will look terrific here. The living room will face here, the kitchen will get the morning sun, and our kids" (who were as yet unborn) "will have so much fun playing in the backyard with all those trees for climbing."

The wife, appearing anxious, responded, "Now, hold on a minute. You are being a little too rash. How do we know the house will even fit on this lot? We don't know if the land is graded properly, if the utilities are hooked up, or if the trees will have to be cut down. We don't even know how much this lot costs or if it's for sale. And frankly, I am still concerned whether we can afford this house at all. I don't think you care at all about our budget."

This conflict is a good example of the differences in *cognitive zones*. A cognitive zone represents the way we gather, evaluate, and act on the information we receive. Since our external environment presents us with an overwhelming amount of information, we need to develop strategies to sort through the volume of data and decide what is important. While there is debate among the researchers as to whether the strategies are determined biologically, environmentally, or some combination of both, there is agreement that individuals develop a preferred approach that shapes the way they process information.

The first dimension of our cognitive zone relates to how we *gather*, or *attend to*, information in our environment, and can be broken down into two different strategies. A *receptive strategy* emphasizes direct observation and firsthand experience. It focuses on facts, details, data, and what is known. Receptive thinkers have few preconceptions about what may be relevant, so they scrutinize all information that they receive. Receptive thinkers are often considered "sensible," "realists," and "practical," and they take a step-by-step approach to problems. An *intuitive strategy*, in contrast, emphasizes concepts, hunches, and the relationships among the various elements of data. The strategy focuses on what could be, rather than on what actually exists. Intuitive thinkers are often considered "visionary," "strategic," or "inspired," and they leap from one challenge to another. Intuitive thinkers focus on the whole, while receptive thinkers focus on the parts of the whole. In our previous example, the husband was an intuitive thinker when he envisioned the possibility of the property, while his wife was a receptive thinker who wanted to make sure all the details were ironed out.

The second dimension of our cognitive zone relates to how we *evaluate* and *decide*. The second dimension can also be broken down into two different strategies. An *analytical strategy* structures information so that decisions can be made in a logical and objective way. It typically is based on a method or process that has a series of systematic steps. Analytical thinkers identify goals and objectives, not the pros and cons of each alternative, and decide impersonally. They are often considered "cool," "just," or "firm but fair" and look to identify the principles involved in the particular situation. The *empathic strategy*, on the other hand, decides in a personal, values-oriented way. The strategy uses logic for the initial evaluation, but bases the ultimate decision on its impact on people. Empathic thinkers often allow decisions to be influenced by their own and others' preferences, and feel rewarded when harmony is achieved and everyone's needs are met. They are often considered "subjective," "merciful," and "compassionate" and look to identify areas of agreement to use as a foundation for decisions.

The final dimension of our cognitive zone relates to how we *act on*, or *respond to*, information in our environment. An *organized strategy* is based on establishing and following a plan of action. Organized thinkers establish goals and objectives and seek quick closure and conclusion so that they can implement the activity. They are often considered "controlling," "decisive," and "organized" and focus on the tasks to be accomplished. A *flexible strategy*, on the other hand, is based on leaving things open for last-minute changes. Flexible thinkers postpone decisions while searching for better options that will allow them to adapt their life to the new information. They are often considered "spontaneous," "curious," and "adaptive" and focus on appreciating the current state or situation.

There is no right or wrong way to gather, decide, and act on information, only preferences. In fact, each strategy within the three dimensions complements the others to provide a total picture of the data that are presented to us. And as with other elements of self-awareness, we do not use just one cognitive strategy. Instead, we fall somewhere on a continuum between the two options within each dimension. A difference in our cognitive zones, however, often intensifies misunderstanding because if we are processing information differently, then we probably perceive different meanings. Awareness of our cognitive zone helps us bridge this gap and sort through these varying perceptions.

Exercise 5: Identify Your Cognitive Zone

Read the two statements in each row. Place a check next to the statement that best describes you.

Column A	Column B
_____ Like the facts.	_____ Like the principles.
_____ Prefer the practical and the realistic.	_____ Prefer the ideal and the possible.
_____ Proceed step by step.	_____ Proceed in bursts of energy.
_____ Prefer the status quo.	_____ Prefer change.
_____ View relationships realistically.	_____ View relationships optimistically.
_____ Patient with detail and routine.	_____ Patient with complications.
_____ Like detailed reports.	_____ Like summary reports.
_____ Trust your experiences.	_____ Trust your hunches.
_____ Communicate literally.	_____ Communicate figuratively.
_____ Like to use standards and procedures.	_____ Like to create new ways to solve problems.
_____ Total	_____ Total

Scoring: Total the number of checks in each column. The score approximates where you fall on the continuum representing the Receptive and Intuitive cognitive strategies, columns A and B, respectively. A score of 10 in one column and 0 in the other represents a strong preference for the strategy receiving ten checks. A score of 5 in one column and 5 in the other represents no preference for either strategy.

Column C	**Column D**
____ Value fair treatment and logic.	____ Value appreciation and understanding.
____ Task-oriented.	____ Relationship-oriented.
____ Prefer to rationally justify your decisions.	____ Prefer to "go with your gut" when making decisions.
____ Truthful.	____ Tactful.
____ Prefer purposeful interactions.	____ Prefer time-consuming interactions.
____ Notice ineffective reasoning.	____ Notice when others need support.
____ Control expressions of love.	____ Offer expressions of love.
____ Cool and unflappable.	____ Warm and passionate.
____ Logical.	____ Sentimental.
____ Just.	____ Merciful.
____ Total	____ Total

Scoring: Use the same procedure as above. Column C represents the Analytical strategy, and column D represents the Empathic strategy.

Column E	**Column F**
____ Prefer a scheduled event.	____ Prefer a spontaneous event.
____ Disciplined and purposeful.	____ Flexible and tolerant.
____ Take immediate action.	____ Take time for reflection.
____ Like reaching conclusions.	____ Like things open-ended.
____ Achievement-oriented.	____ Contingency-oriented.
____ Make lists to direct current activities.	____ Make lists to plan future activities.
____ Results-oriented.	____ Process-oriented.
____ Prefer the stable.	____ Prefer the dynamic.
____ Prefer purpose and direction.	—— Prefer autonomy and versatility.
____ Enjoy work.	____ Enjoy play.
____ Total	____ Total

Scoring: Use the same procedure as above. Column E represents the Organized strategy, and column F represents the Flexible strategy.

Interpersonal Zones and Conflict Resolution

Our interpersonal zones motivate our perceptions and needs. They help us interpret the information we receive from the world around us and establish the basis of our self-concept. When we perceive a challenge to our selves, or to the way *we* define our selves, we naturally become defensive in order to protect our sense of self-esteem. We may be conscious of the challenge, or we may perceive the challenge at a subconscious level. However, when we are in conflict, the defense of our self-esteem has dramatic consequences that thwart our efforts toward constructive resolution.

First, when we defend, we are competing. Defensiveness usually manifests itself as an attack on the other party or as an evasive, protecting maneuver. Either way, we send signals to the other party that demonstrate that we are not currently interested in collaborating, and, depending on the intensity of our attack, we may shift from a discussion of objective issues to personal criticism. Therefore, our reaction to the other party's behavior further escalates the competition and the potential for a destructive interaction.

Second, and more significantly, we greatly increase the likelihood that we will not obtain a favorable outcome for ourselves, regardless of our interest in a positive outcome for the other party. When we defend, we have reprioritized our needs. Thus, we rank our interpersonal needs—the needs that we are defending—higher than the real, more objective issues of the conflict. As a result, we solve the wrong problem.

This is not to discount the value of a strong self-concept, dignity, or emotional self-preservation, but we should not use a conflict as the place to manage our own emotional issues. We should build our self-esteem and self-concept separately from conflicts and disputes because if we let our attacked interpersonal zones determine the solutions, we still may be dissatisfied with the resolution, and will have to revisit the same conflict over and over again.

When you identify your interpersonal zones, you increase your self-awareness and begin to understand how these zones influence—and interfere with—your ability to visualize optimal solutions to your conflicts. As you learn to listen to yourself, you will gain more control of your reactions, which, in turn, will let you listen constructively to the needs of others.

Conclusions

If you do not understand yourself, it is challenging to understand another. Feelings, thoughts, and emotions that churn in our subconscious cloud the communication we receive, and we react without control, without judgment, and without insight. Conflicts go unresolved or we resort to strategies of power and authority that leave others unsatisfied and resentful, and when we are without control, we give in, hoping for vindication the next time. When this occurs, the reasons why we are in conflict remain a mystery.

Self-awareness breaks this action-reaction cycle. It takes us out of the fray, allowing us to see the conflict from a distance, and gives us the power to choose our emotions and behavior. Even if we decide not to change our feelings and actions, we are better able to understand the gaps between our perceptions and the perceptions of others. Knowledge of those differences increases the information available for constructive resolution.

As you begin to increase your self-awareness, pay close attention to the information you receive. Self-assessment is an ongoing process of evaluating the discrepancies between external feedback and your self-concept. When you develop a deeper understanding of yourself, you learn to accept yourself as you are. This allows you to be more accepting of others and have greater confidence in your ability to apply the principles of interaction required for constructive resolution.

3

Principles of Interaction

Nor knowest thou what argument
Thy life to thy neighbor's creed has lent.
All are needed by each one;
Nothing is fair or good alone.

Ralph Waldo Emerson, *Each and All*

Transformation is the result of a willingness to change the rules that govern our behavior. If we want to see different results from our interactions with others, then we must change our conduct and the underlying values that guide our conduct. If we want to see improvement in our ability to manage and resolve the conflicts in our life, we need to cast aside old habits and act in accordance with new principles that will increase our effectiveness.

The *principles of interaction* are a comprehensive and fundamental set of laws that determine how we conduct ourselves with others. They guide our behavior both in and outside of conflict situations, and incorporate both our self-awareness and an awareness of others. These principles serve as the foundation that will transform the technique of listening into a powerful symbol of our underlying character that will open pathways to understanding and resolution. They work together to guide our actions toward constructive interactions. The principles of interaction are:

- Discipline, desire, and patience
- Detached responsibility
- Acceptance
- Mutual gain

Figure 3-1.   Constructive relationship pyramid.

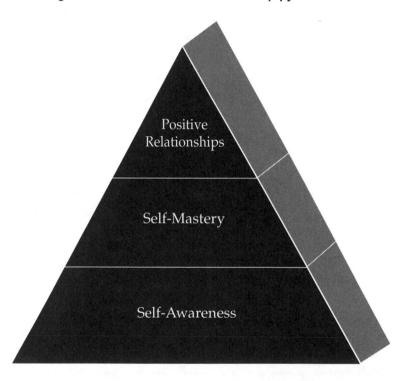

The actress Alla Nazimova once said, "The actor should not play a part. Like the Aeolian harps that used to be hung in the trees to be played only by the breeze, the actor should be an instrument played upon by the character he depicts." In other words, an actor will not master the craft of making a character believable to an audience until he or she lets the character inspire his or her actions. Likewise, we will not be able to resolve conflict constructively until we let our character inspire our actions. The key is building our character upon a set of principles proven to enhance human interaction.

As discussed in Chapter 2, we cannot resolve conflict collaboratively until we have resolved conflict alone, within ourselves. Thus, self-awareness lays the foundation for self-mastery, and self-mastery lays the foundation for productive relationships with others (Figure 3-1). Only when we are able to influence ourselves—to maintain the desire and self-discipline required for change—will we be able to influence others. The principles of interaction help us take what we have learned through self-awareness and cultivate a life philosophy that guides our behavior and helps us listen throughout our conflicts.

Consider the conflict that a mother, Carol, described involving her thirteen-year-old daughter, Jennifer.

Jennifer wanted very badly to go to a concert scheduled to take place on a Saturday night at a coliseum located in the city. Five of Jennifer's friends had already been given the okay by their parents, and they had purchased a ticket for Jennifer. Their plan was to take a thirty-minute train ride into the city, then take a cab or walk the eight blocks to the coliseum. All Jennifer needed was permission from Carol.

Carol was not that enthusiastic about letting her young daughter attend this concert. Transportation issues aside, she was concerned because the coliseum was in a rough part of the city and the musical group was one popular with older, "more experienced" kids. She wanted to demonstrate that she trusted Jennifer's capabilities, but she also wanted to protect her and prevent Jennifer from getting in over her head. She wanted to talk to Jennifer so that they could arrive at a decision that would satisfy both of their interests.

"So, Mom, can I go to this concert?" Jennifer asked.

"I'm not sure yet. I still have some concerns, sweetheart. That coliseum is in a dangerous part of town, you know," said Carol.

"Ah, Mom. All of my friends' parents are letting them go. It can't be all that bad."

"Well, I am not their parents. This is your first time in the city alone." She paused. "And it will be night. You've also never taken the train into the city before. When we go to the city, we usually drive."

"Yeah, but the train seems easy. The other girls have done it before. They'll show me how."

"But you are a bunch of thirteen-year-old girls."

"Thirteen! Thirteen! When I'm sixteen I won't be old enough! Mom, it's not fair. All the other girls are going. There will be six of us! I know what you want. You want us to have a chaperon. But if we brought a parent along, it just wouldn't look cool. We'd be the only kids there with their parents."

"Well, I don't care about cool. And I just don't think you should go."

"But Mom."

"No buts, young lady. I'm your mother, and I'm looking out for your best interests."

This type of conflict may sound familiar to many of us, and it is an example of destructive conflict resolution. Jennifer's interest was to be part of the group attending the show, whereas Carol's interest was to share her concerns and then come up with a solution that would satisfy them both. Had the conflict taken a more constructive turn, they might have identified a number of solutions that could satisfy their interests. For example, one solution might have been to have a parent drive the girls to the concert and pick them up after it was over (of course, the trip would be taken in the family minivan, thus causing additional embarrassment to the girls). Another solution could have been to have a parent purchase a ticket to the show in a different part of the coliseum. That way there would be someone available in case of an emergency.

There were many other possibilities that would satisfy Jennifer's desire to attend the concert while maintaining her independence and satisfy Carol's interest in Jennifer's safety. However, the solutions were not important. The fact that there are many options that would satisfy both parties should prove this. Therefore, the resolution ultimately is not as important as the *process* that leads to resolution—the interaction that allows the solutions to appear. Carol failed to create that environment; instead, she reacted emotionally and resorted to using her authority, a destructive, competitive tactic. The subtle lesson that she taught Jennifer was, "Use your power to get your way." Carol lost her self-awareness and lost an opportunity to create a positive process.

As the going gets tough during conflict and we appear to move farther away from resolution, we often begin to dust off the trusty, old destructive strategies we have used in the past to get our win. Like Carol, we may *compete* by using power and authority to get our way. We also may use other competitive tactics, such as misinformation or manipulation. For example, Jennifer used misinformation by saying that all the other parents were letting their kids attend the concert. Carol later found out that only three parents had given the okay; the other two girls were not going to tell their parents. Jennifer also used manipulation when she brought up being "cool." In past conflicts, she had discovered that "cool" was a hot zone for Carol, who wanted her daughter to maintain status within her peer group, since, as Carol confided, she "wasn't very cool as a kid" because her mother was "oppressive." As the conflict intensifies, we also may choose to *accommodate,* or give in. For example, had Carol succumbed to her hot zone, "cool," she probably would have let Jennifer go to the concert. She would have prioritized her own need to be cool—through her daughter—above her need to protect Jennifer. Finally, we also may choose to *avoid* the conflict; had Jennifer stormed off to her room—as she had in past disputes—she would have used this strategy. Neither Carol nor Jennifer used *collaboration* to manage the conflict constructively.

Behavior rewarded is behavior repeated. The "win" that Carol achieved in this dispute reinforced her use of competitive strategies when the first attempts at collaboration proved too challenging. Past wins for each of them also rewarded the use of accommodation and avoidance. The three destructive orientations have become their comfort zones, but they also have begun to weaken the foundation of the relationship. The destructive strategies may resolve the objective issues of the conflict, but over the long term they intensify the personal issues that ultimately create a barrier of effective interaction.

Collaboration is not easy. In fact, of the four orientations to conflict, it is the most difficult to maintain because it requires self-mastery. It requires that we manage the emotions that cause us to react destructively during a dispute. If we want to keep conflict constructive, then we must master the first principle of interaction: *discipline, desire, and patience.*

Discipline, Desire, and Patience

We all have a tendency to avoid things that are unpleasant. After all, given the choice between something pleasurable, say an afternoon enjoying our favorite leisure activity, and something unpleasant, such as cleaning our attic, we would most likely choose to enjoy an afternoon of fun. That's normal. However, we also know that when we put off doing unpleasant tasks, they have a tendency to become much bigger problems down the road. If we never clean our attic, the junk piles up and we eventually run out of storage space. Then, cleaning takes much longer than if we had organized the space along the way.

Conflict is no different from many of the other unpleasant tasks in life. The longer we delay dealing with it head on, the more trouble we will have reaching resolution. This is particularly true with conflict because the personal issues—the "junk," if you will—of conflict have a tendency to pile up into resentment and contempt that block the more easily organized objective issues. Nevertheless, we often avoid confronting conflict because it generates uncomfortable emotions, such as frustration, hurt, and pain. Even if we have confronted conflict, maintaining a constructive, collaborative orientation throughout the interaction is difficult and time-consuming, and it interferes with activities that are more pleasurable. It is simpler and more expedient to model Carol's behavior and choose another strategy to end, at least temporarily, the painful and stressful interaction.

Discipline is the principle of interaction that helps us deal with unpleasant activities. It reminds us to continue down the path of collaboration no matter how painful and challenging the process may become. It keeps us focused on our objective—constructive resolution—even when the other party becomes insulting, competitive, and destructive. Without discipline, we risk giving in to the temptation to choose other, less challenging strategies for resolution that usually produce unacceptable results for one or both parties. With discipline, we confront and persevere.

Confronting our disputes and sustaining a productive resolution process is much easier if we truly have the *desire* to collaborate. In other words, if we want to achieve positive outcomes, we have to be motivated by a strong need to resolve conflict constructively. However, if desire is to be a principle of interaction, it must be motivated by the right factors. We may desire to end the dispute, but that is different from desiring a collaborative outcome. We might also desire to achieve a favorable outcome for ourselves, but that may ignore the other party's interests and needs. We may even want to resolve the conflict constructively, but not unless the other person first changes her or his attitude or behavior. None of these examples represents desire for constructive conflict resolution, and without desire, no amount of discipline will favorably affect the dispute.

The final element of the first principle of interaction is *patience*. You may be disciplined and willing to confront the conflict. You may also have the desire for a constructive resolution. But unless you are willing to let the interaction take its natural course, you are likely to fall back on destructive habits. Patience is the willingness to wait it out. It requires that you keep a big-picture perspective and recognize that some of the parties to the conflict have not developed effective conflict-management skills and need more time to work through their issues and needs.

Consider the example of Steve, the general manager of a small manufacturing facility. He described his plant as a rough-and-tumble place where the employees, who were poorly educated and came from lower-income backgrounds, tended to resolve their disputes through heated arguments and occasional brawls. In one three-month period, for example, a dozen fights erupted among his fifty to sixty employees.

Steve wanted to change the culture in the facility, but he soon realized that not all of the blame belonged to his employees. He recognized that he had to change his style if he wanted to see changes in their orientation. A hulking fellow of 6'4" and over 275 pounds, Steve typically resolved conflict through intentional, and sometimes unintentional, intimidation. He had been big all his life, and this strategy, while destructive, had been effective in helping him get his way. However, he knew that he would have to model constructive resolution if he really wanted to change the culture, and over the course of a few months, he tried to master the principles of interaction while also working diligently on his listening skills.

Early one morning, an angry employee stormed into his office, slammed the door, pushed a chair out of the way, and hit Steve squarely in the chin. Steve got up off the floor, rubbed his chin, and said, "It seems as if you are angry."

The employee stomped his feet, yelled, and cursed, and Steve responded calmly, "It sounds like [the incident] is important to you, and you are frustrated because I [interfered without consulting with you]."

Within a few moments, the employee calmed down, apologized for hitting Steve, and began to talk about the objective issues. An hour or so later, they reached a mutually acceptable resolution and went back to work.

When asked later why he did not fire the employee on the spot for the violent outburst, Steve's response was, "I realized that my guys have pretty poor language and interpersonal skills, and most of them haven't yet learned how to express their emotions any other way except through outbursts. If I was ever going to get them to change their behavior, I had to demonstrate—I mean really demonstrate—that they could confront me to try to solve problems they had with me. I don't like getting slugged, but it sent the message that I was willing to work with them."

That is discipline, desire, and patience. This is not to suggest that hitting and violence should be tolerated; rather, it shows the results of applying the principles of interaction even when the situation might compel us to abandon them. Steve could have "won" that dispute by using his authority as plant manager to fire the employee, but he realized that that would have demonstrated the wrong *intention*. Instead, he wanted to embody his goal of tolerance, understanding, and support. Had he fired the employee, he would have sent the opposite message. By exercising discipline, desire, and patience, he demonstrated how self-awareness can lead to self-mastery and that no conflict could make him lose sight of his objective.

Discipline, desire, and patience enhance our interactions by confronting and sustaining the constructive process. They help us stick to our game plan even though it appears that it is not yet working. It is trusting your system and maintaining a self-awareness that clarifies our intentions and priorities, and breaks the action-reaction cycle.

Detached Responsibility

We cannot solve conflict without taking responsibility for the resolution. Yet, we cannot begin to act interdependently, to become self-aware, and to resolve the conflict we encounter until we have detached from the situation. How can we both take responsibility and stay detached? How can we control and give up control? That is the yin and yang of *detached responsibility* and the second principle of interaction.

What Is Attachment?

Mary Beth worked as a nurse for a family practitioner and was miserable. She complained that her boss, Dr. Stromm, was unfair and abusive. She said that he constantly criticized her ability in front of patients and staff, and poked fun at everything from her southern accent to her weight. Although she first accepted this with a "good sense of humor," eventually, she began arguing with him about it. According to Mary Beth, he even remarked that her "primary problem was that [Mary Beth] isn't pretty enough to work in this office."

At first, Mary Beth attributed the behavior to the pressure of running a medical office or to family difficulties. Her initial response was to work harder and to try to help him feel better about her and the office. She even volunteered to baby-sit so that he and his wife could get the time alone that they needed.

However, the problem persisted, and eventually she became more anxious about the situation. She worried so much about making a mistake at work that she made more mistakes than ever. Her family and friends also noticed that the only thing she could talk about was her situation with Dr. Stromm. She rushed home to report every incident that occurred during the day and was unable to quit talking or thinking about her problem.

In addition, Mary Beth reported radical swings in her behavior at the office. One minute she was trying to be pleasant, the next she was crying, and the next she exploded for no significant reason. Not only was the situation with Dr. Stromm deteriorating, but other employees were finding it hard to work with her as well. Mary Beth blamed everyone at the office for contributing to the matter, as she worried what the doctor was going to do or say next. She had trouble sleeping, and she put on weight. She wanted to quit, but she was afraid that quitting was only running away from the conflict. She wanted the situation to improve, but she expected Dr. Stromm to take responsibility for the improvement by "fixing his character flaws."

Mary Beth was attached. She was so involved with the conflict that she could not separate herself from the problem. Like many of us, she fell victim to the dependent-independent cycle of reactions to the dispute. She vacillated between wanting someone else to solve the problem and wanting to solve the problem alone, without interacting with the doctor.

Attachment occurs when we worry, obsess, and remain preoccupied with a problem or person. It also occurs when we try to control all aspects of the people and problems in our environment, or when we try to save the situation or provide the answers. We are attached when we lose our self-awareness and react to the hot zones within disputes, when we let people or situations get to us. We are fully attached when we are no longer aware of ourselves as separate from the person, the situation, or the damage caused by both, and we link our happiness or unhappiness to whether they meet our growing expectations of them.

Studies have demonstrated that when we are attached, or overly committed to someone or something in this dysfunctional way, we often do not work out the best solutions to conflict

(Kelley and Schenitzki, 1972; Fry, Firestone, and Williams, 1979). There is evidence that attachment clouds our understanding of the needs of both parties. Also, we are likely to shift from fighting the other party to extreme acquiescence. We are likely to accommodate in the extreme and arrive at a resolution that we resent over the long term.

When we are attached, we also give others the power to avoid resolution. We give them permission to give up responsibility for their part in the problem-solving process. What began as a problem caused by the abusive comments of Dr. Stromm, for example, shifted to a problem intensified by Mary Beth's reaction to the comments. Eventually, Dr. Stromm was able to blame the extended conflict on her behavior, her lack of control, not himself.

We cannot resolve conflict constructively if we are attached because the relationship becomes entangled with the problem. Every conflict involves both objective issues and personal issues, and these must be addressed separately if the parties in conflict are going to reach resolution. If we cannot distinguish between the two different types of issues, then we begin to see all problems as personal attacks. For example, "the chart was not filled out correctly" became intertwined with "you are unattractive." While the doctor may have been cruel and abusive personally, he also had a legitimate performance issue. Mary Beth's attachment, however, prevented her from treating each comment individually. Consequently, the conflict eroded into a competitive battle of wills that was ultimately won by the party with the most power and authority—the doctor.

What Is Detached Responsibility?

Detached responsibility is the ability to resolve conflict by separating the objective issues of a dispute from the personal issues. It is the process of managing the aspects of the conflict that are within your control while, as Roger Fisher and William Ury suggest in their book *Getting to Yes*, "separating the people from the problem" (1981). It means that if we are going to achieve constructive resolution, we need to take *responsibility* for the conflict—*our* part of the conflict.

We have to accept responsibility for a problem before we can solve it. We cannot solve a problem by saying, "It's not my problem" or "It's their problem." We cannot solve a problem by hoping that someone else will come to our rescue. The interdependence inherent in conflict requires accepting at least partial responsibility because we do not want to be dependent on the other party's solution and we cannot solve the conflict alone.

When we say it is someone else's problem, we are avoiding conflict—and pain. That is inconsistent with the first principle of interaction: discipline, desire, and patience. We avoid our responsibility if we say that someone else caused the problem and that it is up to him or her to solve it. We give away power if we say that the circumstances are beyond our control. Therefore, we must accept responsibility for resolving the problem. But as we have seen, accepting responsibility can go too far and end up as attachment—obsession and worry that have no impact on the outcome. Instead, we must practice *detached* responsibility.

Detachment is the process of distancing ourselves from the relationship. It does not mean that we end the relationship in anger, nor does it mean we resign ourselves to accept the conflict. Detachment means that we learn what we can control and what we cannot. It is based on the notion that people are responsible for themselves and are free to make their own choices, whether we like them or not. When we detach, we stop trying to control or influence other people's choices and we take back the ability to make our own.

Detached responsibility is *taking control of what you can control*—your own thoughts, actions, and behavior—and *letting go of the things you cannot control*. It is an acceptance of reality as opposed to a focus on the ideal. We stop saying, "He should," "She should," or "If only." Instead, we say, "I can," "I will," and "Next time."

In the above example, Mary Beth could detach responsibility by recognizing that she had no control over whether Dr. Stromm insulted her or not and no control over how he evaluated her job performance. She had control over her reactions to his comments, and she had the ability to let him know that the comments were unacceptable. She also had control over her ability to perform the job the best she could and, ultimately, over her decision to continue working at that office. If he chose to insult her, she could exercise one of her options and ignore the comments, confront him, or resign.

When Should We Detach?

We usually do not realize when we are attached. By then, we are obsessing about a dispute, failing to separate the objective issues from the personal issues, and creating additional interpersonal conflict that interferes with constructive resolution. But it is still not too late to detach. As Melody Beattie suggests in *Codependent No More* (1987), we should detach when,

> We can't stop thinking, talking about, or worrying about, someone or something; when our emotions are churning and boiling; when we feel like we have to do something about someone because we can't stand it another minute; when we're hanging on by a thread, and it feels like that single thread is frayed; and when we believe we can no longer live with the problem we've been trying to live with. . . . A good rule of thumb is: You need to detach most when it seems the least likely or possible thing to do.

We need to maintain detached responsibility all the time. We should enter our interactions with detached responsibility whether we are in conflict or not. In fact, detached responsibility will help prevent objective conflicts from becoming personal. It will help us maintain a constructive, collaborative approach to all conflicts we encounter.

How Do We Detach Responsibly?

Dennis McKnight, of the Center for Cognitive Behavior Therapy in Greensboro, North Carolina, provides a valuable metaphor that helps to illustrate detached responsibility. Imagine that each of us is an island, and we each have the responsibility for maintaining our own island. We need to cut the grass, trim the bushes, and dispose of the trash. But sometimes it is more satisfying, or more fun, to jump over onto someone else's island and show that person the blades of grass they missed, the bushes that still need trimming, or the trash that clutters the environment. Sometimes, we even do the work.

What we fail to realize, however, is that maybe the other party prefers the length of the grass and the natural look of the bushes. And maybe the trash does not bother her or him that much. And besides, the person asks, "Why are you telling me to fix my island, when yours is not in great shape?" He or she tells us to go back to our own island and fix our own problems. We have just created a personal conflict because, in a sense, we told the person that he or she didn't measure up to our standards.

Nevertheless, we like to "help" other people manage their islands. We feel good about fixing their problems. It boosts our self-esteem. This is especially true if our island is a mess because it is much easier to point out problems on other islands than it is to take care of the problems on our own. Taking care of our own islands requires discipline, desire, and patience. When we interfere with other islands, we ignore the boundaries between islands and attach ourselves to a problem. In contrast, detached responsibility is managing your island—only your island—and leaving the other islands to manage themselves.

Detached responsibility does not mean that we stop caring for other people. On the contrary, we care so much that we promise not to interfere unless they ask for our help. And then, we will offer our help only when we are sure they really want it, and only when we are sure that we can maintain the boundaries. Being detached does not mean that we will accommodate and let people have their way while not satisfying our needs. But it does mean that we will prevent them from manipulating our emotions. It does not mean, for example, that Carol would let Jennifer waltz off to the concert. Instead, Carol would not be affected by her hot zones and would keep the personal issues separate from the objective concerns of the dispute.

Of the two parts of detached responsibility, it is harder to detach. Most of us are comfortable with responsibility. After all, responsibility gives us a feeling of self-worth, of value, of making a difference. However, we resist detaching because we often have a lot invested in the object of our attachment. We have worked hard to achieve this high degree of conflict, and we do not want to let go now! Detachment is difficult, too, because we have to trust the other person or the situation to find a solution, although our experience has shown us that we cannot do so. With every freedom comes a responsibility, and with every decision comes a consequence. Give others permission to take responsibility for themselves and accept their own consequences. We have to be willing to let go and trust.

The following four steps outline how to maintain detached responsibility:

1. *Recognize what you can control.* You can control your perceptions and your thoughts about those perceptions. You can control your reactions and your thoughts about the reactions of others. Separate the objective issues from the personal issues.
2. *Control it!* Increase your self-awareness and understand your interpersonal zones. Manage your island. Stop criticizing yourself. Be accepting.
3. *Recognize what you cannot control.* You cannot control other people, you can only hope to influence them. You cannot control the variety of situations that you encounter; you can only control your reactions to those situations.
4. *Let go!* Accept reality. Maintain boundaries. Create an alternative.

Acceptance

Detachment helps us recognize that a person's unacceptable behavior often demonstrates a lack of self-awareness of the hot zones that cause the person to react destructively in conflict. Discipline, desire, and patience keep us focused on the good and potentially likeable person that lies underneath. Together, they provide the foundation for *acceptance,* the ability to see the world as it is without judgment or condemnation. To demonstrate acceptance, two important skills are required:

1. Separate the person from the behavior.
2. Welcome their perspective.

Separate the Person From the Behavior

Acceptance is the difference between liking the other party as a human being and liking her or his behavior and actions. We often cannot accept someone's behavior. For example, we might not like it when an employee is consistently late, when a family member leaves the living room a mess, or, at a different level, when someone calls us a "stupid jerk." However, if these individuals were self-aware, would they be likely to make these choices? Would they intentionally disregard our needs and choose to hurt our feelings or insult us? If they would—if they would *consciously and intentionally* disregard their interdependence with us—then it is unlikely that they will collaborate. If they are that devious, it is unlikely that our listening-based conflict management skills will ever work.

However, remember the opening line from Chapter 2, "Hatred against oneself is inseparable from hatred against others." If other people disregard, insult, abuse, or hurt us in the interaction, they are probably in pain themselves. There is something going on inside of them, some past or present hurt, or some conflict between their rational and emotional minds that they have not resolved. Moreover, when their self-concept is that shaky, they have to defend their actions—no matter how bad they may be—in order to feel better about themselves. This becomes a self-perpetuating downward cycle unless something, or someone, breaks them out of this pattern of behavior.

"Well," you say, "their problems are not *my* responsibility. They should grow up, act like adults, and stop this behavior!" You are right. You do not have to deal with their problems. However, if you do not, do not expect to achieve a constructive resolution. In these cases, we will have to seek an alternative (discussed further in Chapter 6). But how many times have we said something *we* later regretted because we were temporarily *un*-self-aware? It is not easy to always be self-aware and recognize your interdependence with the other party, is it?

As we develop self-awareness, however, we begin to recognize that we do not just feel lousy around the other person. We become aware of the specific behavior that makes us feel lousy. If we can see the behavior, then we can separate the behavior from the person's unaware self. Once we peel away the layers of unaware behavior, we are left with a decent human being. In some cases, there might not be much that remains, but there is a human being somewhere in there that is worthy of acceptance.

If we say, "I do not like your behavior," we are not demonstrating acceptance. If we say, "I do not like how I *feel* because of your behavior," we are detached responsibly and on our way to acceptance. Others can choose to behave however they wish. How we *feel* about their behavior is our problem, not theirs. We can feel any way we choose because we are self-aware and in control. When we see that others are not in control of themselves, it is easier to separate the person from the behavior and demonstrate acceptance.

Imagine a four-year-old child coming up to us and saying, "You're a stinky dumb-dumb. I hate you!" What is our reaction? We might admonish the child for using unacceptable language. We might be disappointed or even a little hurt. However, we would probably recognize that the child did not know any better. At that age, children do not have the self-control to manage their emotions and their outbursts. We most likely would quickly forgive the child and try to understand the problem. We would show support. We would give him or her a hug.

However, when a forty-year-old adult says the grown-up equivalent of "stinky dumb dumb," why do we react differently? We react differently because this person is an adult and should know better, right? Furthermore, how dare he or she say that to us! If that is our response, then we need to consider two important points. First, we are *not* detached responsibly and managing our reaction to the other person's behavior. Second, are most people really that much more in control at age forty than they were at age four? Maybe . . . if only . . . they should be.

Acceptance requires that we see reality without judgment. This does not mean that we must adapt permanently to the existing conditions, nor does it mean that we have to tolerate abuse. It does mean that we acknowledge the current circumstances as they, and we, are. Only from this perspective will we have the clarity to begin to understand and evaluate the situation, engage in constructive conflict resolution, and solve our problems. If we remain attached, angry, or in denial of our current reality, then we will not have the peace of mind required to collaborate. We will not exercise detached responsibility, or be able to maintain discipline, desire, and patience. To help you separate the person from the behavior, consider the following questions.

- What are the behaviors, actions, comments, or situations that are bothering you?
- Why do these behaviors, actions, comments, or situations bother you? What is the impact on you?
- How do you feel about it? What emotions are generated? (If you feel angry, try to identify the emotion that generated the anger. For example, the person *hurt* your feelings, and that makes you angry; or she *embarrassed* you, and that makes you angry.)
- Why did the person act that way? What is going on in his or her emotional mind to create the situation? How do you think the person feels from her or his perspective?
- Why might the person lack trust? Why might he or she feel out of control? Why might he or she feel disrespected?
- How does the person perceive you? Why?

Welcome Their Perspective

The second part of acceptance is agreeing that other people's thoughts, feelings, and needs are justified from their perspective. This does not necessarily mean that we universally or unconditionally agree with them. Instead, it means that given their current reality, their perspective has merit. It is walking a mile in the other person's shoes. Welcoming their perspective does not mean that you must deny your own perspective, for denial is judgmental and evaluative. Welcoming their perspective means that you expand your perspective to *include* their information (Figure 3-2).

The danger in this second element of acceptance, however, is that you risk being criticized directly and indirectly by the other person. None of us likes to be criticized because it often leads to misunderstanding and hurt feelings. For example, think of a time during the past few weeks when someone's criticism got to you. Did your boss imply that you were not doing a good job? Did a coworker make you feel defensive? Did your spouse confront you with an old habit you were not ready to change? We all struggle with accepting criticism at one time or another, but the principle of acceptance requires that we welcome it.

Figure 3-2.   Welcome their perspective: pieces of the puzzle.

Our
Perspective

Their
Perspective

Just as criticism can cause problems, it also can help us identify the ways in which we are interdependent. When we listen to
another party's anger, hurt, and criticism without becoming defensive, we contribute significantly to constructive resolution.
We hear how that person *needs us* to resolve the dispute, and her
or his feedback provides one of the most vital resources we have
for collaboration.

To make criticism work for us, however, we have to go beyond positional defensiveness. The reason we often react defen-
sively when criticized is that we feel personally attacked. Our
anger is less about the information we have received, and more
about who is right, who is in control, and who has the final authority. In these situations, we feel misunderstood, and we do
not want to give in. When we become defensive, we are engaged
in a competitive battle of wills with the other party that is based
more on defending our respective self-concepts than on resolving the specific issues that are raised.

If we give up insisting how right we are and try to listen to
understand other people's perspectives, we allow those people
to be right as well, and we give them emotional space to communicate their thoughts and needs. On the other hand, the more
we insist how wrong they are, the more they will try to prove
their point, and the more we take away the emotional space they
may need to build their self-esteem. Typically, people have a
need to prove their point when their sense of self-worth is tied to
being right. *We* do not need to prove that we are right, because
our self-concept is stronger than that. If our self-esteem is low,
however, we need to work on it outside of the conflict-resolution
process. Otherwise, personal issues will become intermingled
with objective issues and increase the chances of a destructive
interaction.

When we demonstrate acceptance, our intention is to help
others feel more relaxed, appreciated, and understood. Empathic
listening, explained more fully in Chapter 4, is the key to establishing this environment. We are not demonstrating acceptance
when we are impatient with their communication, interrupt as
they are speaking, or refuse to give in, even if their perspective
makes sense. We also indicate a lack of acceptance if we make
others feel guilty, stupid, or uncomfortable. As soon as they

show signs of defensiveness, we must shift toward doing those things that restore the constructive environment.

One way to help other people get beyond name calling and to demonstrate that we accept their thoughts is to *reframe* their statements. Reframing is the process of turning a criticism into a problem to be solved collaboratively. For example, suppose a coworker criticizes us by saying, "I can never trust you!" Our instinct would be to come back with, "That's not true! You can trust me." We have just created a competition in which he would provide an example proving that he cannot trust us and we would provide an example showing him that he was wrong. We would get nowhere. Instead, we should reframe by saying, "I am sorry because I want to be trustworthy. Help me understand what I need to do for you to trust me."

When we reframe, we shift the focus of the argument away from positions and toward identifying the needs and interests that will lead toward resolution. We also might ask for more information that will ensure that we know what this person really means by "trustworthy." Maybe he really means that he cannot "count on our follow-through" or "does not feel supported." These issues may be different from "trust." Reframing helps us properly diagnose the problem.

Reframing also helps us establish a common objective. Instead of turning the criticism into an either-or, competitive battle, we work together to identify criteria for solutions. This provides remarkable *validation* that the other party's thoughts and needs are important to you and shifts that party's attention away from the hot zones expressed by the criticism. As we build others' self-esteem, they are more likely to engage in constructive behavior.

When we welcome their perspective, we not only create an environment that encourages positive interaction, but also acquire more tools to help us explore solutions to our conflicts. We expand our view of the dispute by allowing the other party to reveal her or his true needs. This information will help us understand both the nature of our common objectives and the specific interests we must help the other party satisfy in order to achieve mutual gain. The following questions will help you identify how to welcome another's perspective:

- Why am I right?
- Why is he or she right?
- Why are we both right?
- Why are we both wrong?
- Why does this conflict not matter?
- How can I reframe his or her perspective to establish a common objective?

Mutual Gain

A purchasing director for an industrial manufacturing company once explained to a group of colleagues attending a conference how he had brought a new, tougher negotiating strategy to his organization. He described using a variety of competitive tactics, including making excessive demands, playing "Good Guy–Bad Guy," using decoys and red herrings, and limiting the amount of information he was willing to share with his "opponents." He bragged that suppliers now feared the company because he was able to drive hard bargains and always get his "win."

A number of those nearby sat in awe listening to him tell his tales until one individual asked quite innocently, "How do you know when you've obtained the best deal possible?"

The purchasing director flashed a big smile, leaned back in his chair, crossing his hands behind his neck, and said, "When I've created such small margins for them that they go out of business."

What machismo! What bravado! What utter lunacy! A year later he was fired from the company.

Remember our definition of conflict as the competition between *interdependent* parties who perceive that they have incompatible needs, goals, desires, or ideas. Interdependence implies that we need each other in some way. We each have something the other wants, whether it is a product, service, support, or acceptance. We need to trade. We need to negotiate. We need each other to survive so that we can continue the exchange. In fact, we need each other to flourish so that we can ease the burden of the interaction.

The purchasing director missed the point. He failed to recognize the interdependence of those interactions. His approach later cost his company hundreds of thousands of dollars when it ran out of suppliers willing to do business with the organization and was stuck with expensive sole-source suppliers that held the company hostage. By ignoring the inherent interdependence, he won in the short term, but missed the longer-term opportunity for larger mutual gain.

The fourth principle of interaction, *mutual gain,* suggests that unless both parties in conflict benefit from the interaction, they should find alternative solutions to satisfy their needs (the concept of alternative solutions is outlined in Chapter 6). This is win-win thinking in which all parties find final agreements satisfactory and are committed to the action plan. Mutual gain is cooperative, collaborative, and constructive. It is principled conflict resolution that is based on satisfying common needs and interests by creating a variety of acceptable options for solving the problems of the dispute. It is beyond positional thinking and recognizes that constructive resolution is not about your way or my way. Mutual gain is focused on a better way

Mutual gain is a principle of interaction precisely because it requires a *change* in our existing or natural conduct. Collaboration goes against our predisposition as humans. Remember that competition is biologically programmed into us and reinforced by many cultural norms. Social-psychological research even has demonstrated that given opportunities to cooperate, people choose competition (Luce and Raiffa, 1957).

The Prisoner's Dilemma Game

The classic Prisoner's Dilemma game provides a wonderful metaphor for our competitive nature by showing that even when two parties would benefit from collaboration, they still make competitive choices. A variation of the game is set up so that you and a stranger are in separate rooms, and in front of each of you are two buttons, one black and the other red. Your task is simply to push one of these buttons. Depending upon the choices made by both you and the other person, you will each win or lose an amount of money, as follows: if you both push black, you will each win one dollar; if you both push red, you will each lose one dollar; and if one pushes red while the other pushes black, the one who pressed the red button will win two dollars while the one who pressed the black button will lose two dollars (Figure 3-3).

As you might expect, when pairs of strangers are asked to play the game just once, they tend to act less cooperatively than when they play the game repeatedly. This is because they know that they cannot be held accountable for their behavior and are therefore more willing to attempt to exploit the other by choosing red. Both players tend to choose red, and both lose. When the game is played over a series of successive turns, and each player is told the other's choice at the end of each turn, cooperation is more likely, although it tends to eventually deteriorate.

Figure 3-3.   Prisoner's dilemma outcomes.

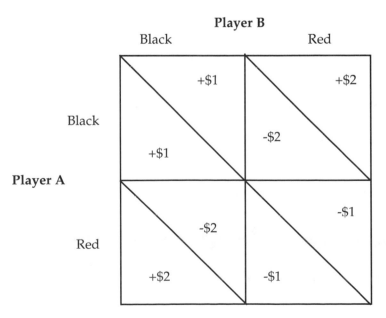

If Player A and Player B begin the game without prior information about each other, they often start by choosing black on the first turn. In other words, they show a willingness to trust each other and a desire to be trustworthy. The result is mutually beneficial, since they both receive $1. Once they have established this kind of cooperative relationship, they typically maintain it for quite some time. After a while, however, one person—A, for example—is tempted to take an action that maximizes his return although it costs the other person. Further, having done this once, A is likely to continue the competitive behavior, perhaps thinking that B will look upon it as a mistake and not change her previously established pattern. Player A chooses this path because he becomes more greedy, competitive, or even just plain bored.

However, Player B responds quickly, and for the next several turns, a mutually competitive pattern is established. Occasionally, one of the pair attempts a heroic action to break the competitive cycle and indicate to the other party that he or she is willing to accept a loss in order to get them both to a winning position. This may succeed for the short run, but eventually the pair slips back into a pattern of mutually competitive, costly behavior (Figure 3-4).

Researchers have elicited vastly different behaviors on the part of the two players by varying the introduction to the Prisoner's Dilemma game. When the players are told that they are in a competitive game and that their goal is to get a higher score than their partner, the participants usually end up selecting the red red combination (1/-1). On the other hand, when the game is positioned as a collaborative game, in which each player is supposed to try to help the other win as much as possible, the players usually finish in the black-black square (+1/+1). Finally, when the game is presented as individualistic, with each player supposed to try to get the highest score without regard for the other's wins or losses, there is greater variability in behavior, although the players typically end up in the red-red square more often than not (Bixenstine, Lowenfeld, and Englehart, 1981; Scodel, Minas, Ratoosh, and Lipetz, 1959; Deutsch, 1958).

Figure 3-4.   Prisoner's dilemma choices.

| | Player A | | Player B | |
Turn	Choice	Outcome	Choice	Outcome
1	Black	+1	Black	+1
2	Black	+1	Black	+1
3	Black	+1	Black	+1
4	Red	+2	Black	-2
5	Red	-1	Red	-1
6	Red	-1	Red	-1
7	Red	-1	Red	-1
8	Black	-2	Red	+2
9	Black	-2	Red	+2
10	Red	+2	Black	-2
11	Red	-1	Red	-1
12	Red	-1	Red	-1

Factors Creating Mutual Gain

Constructive conflict resolution requires that we collaborate to reach mutual gain. The Prisoner's Dilemma game, however, demonstrates that it is difficult to shift from a competitive to a cooperative orientation. A number of factors have been shown to influence the outcomes of the Prisoner's Dilemma game toward collaboration, and they provide a good model to demonstrate the requirements of mutual gain.

1. *Open communication.* Open communication significantly helps to shift the situation from competition to collaboration. In the previous example, the parties communicated through their actions. However, if the communication is spoken or written, it can help the parties jump more quickly into a collaborative mode because it establishes acknowledged commitment to the strategy. So, if after Turn 4, Player B had said, "If you continue to choose red, I also will choose red. But if you choose black, I also

will choose black," Player A would most likely have chosen to cooperate on the next turn.

The way we communicate also is important. For instance, communications containing promises are more effective than those containing threats (Tedeschi, Bonoma, and Brown, 1971). Threats are often perceived as hostile, competitive acts, and once hostility and the resulting distrust have entered the relationship, they are extremely difficult to eliminate. Therefore, the more open communication and trust are established up front, before we lose control of our emotions and react with threats, the more likely it is that the relationship will sustain the collaborative environment. Communication that is supportive and nonjudgmental also seems to have an impact. For example, saying, "We might consider working together on the next turn," would have a more positive effect than, "It's unfair when you compete!"

Open communication enhances trust and the willingness to share information. Although we may see things differently, if we are communicating openly and are willing to listen to each other, we demonstrate that we are willing to try to establish outcomes that are satisfactory to both of us. Even if the other party has a competitive or individualistic orientation, when we communicate openly and demonstrate the principles of interaction, we gradually break down the competitive walls and build trust that strengthens the collaborative relationship.

2. *Attitude of abundance.* A critical factor affecting our ability to shift the other party from a competitive orientation to the principle of mutual gain is each party's perception of the available resources. Built into our genetic programming is the notion that there are limited food supplies, limited breeding grounds, and limited spaces in which to build our homes. This *attitude of limits* is what compels us to stake out as much territory for ourselves as we can without regard for others in our environment. Combined with a poor self-concept, it also is what makes it difficult for us to enjoy the success of other people, regardless of the degree of success that we enjoy. If they "win," it must mean that we "lose." Therefore, in the Prisoner's Dilemma metaphor, it is difficult to watch the other party consistently "win" $1 because, although we also win $1, we see it as not winning $2.

The principle of mutual gain requires that we maintain an *attitude of abundance,* which suggests that there are plenty of resources for everybody. Abundance comes from a strong sense of self that is not challenged by the success or acquired resources of others and is not defined by a comparative and ever-changing pecking order. An attitude of abundance defines success on the basis of whether both parties' interests are satisfied. In contrast, an attitude of limits defines success on the basis of whether positional, either-or demands have been met. This sets up a win-lose or zero-sum game. Either we get what we want or we lose. The alternative, an attitude of abundance, sees the value in going beyond positions to recognize the abundant ways of satisfying the interests of both parties.

An attitude of abundance was displayed during a conflict between a product manager and a chief financial officer for a consumer products company. During a particularly tight financial period, the CFO required that all departments reduce their budgets by 15 percent. This was distressing to the product manager, since she needed an increase in her budget in order to implement a potentially lucrative product launch. She could not understand why the CFO was so "shortsighted" and willing to risk revenue growth—the very thing the company needed to improve financially—by forgoing the expenditures required for implementation.

Initially, they each staked out a position and tried to convince and persuade the other into compliance. Upon further dialogue, however, they realized that the 15 percent reduction was really the average reduction needed in order to achieve the financial targets. The CFO suggested that the product manager could increase her budget as much as she needed, as long as other departments were willing to reduce their budgets more than 15 percent. Since many of the other departments were involved in the planning process for the new product introduction, they were happy to find additional savings that provided for her increase. An attitude of abundance helped the CFO and product manager reframe the conflict and satisfy the competing needs.

3. *Common interests and goals.* Another significant way to affect the amount of collaboration displayed is to highlight the in-

terdependence of the two parties. If one party takes a competitive position, it is up to the other party to demonstrate acceptance and reframe the position as an interest that establishes a common goal. Positional demands are often a display of defensiveness and are the natural reaction to feeling overwhelmed by the interaction. By establishing common interests and goals, or creating positive goals interdependence, we diffuse the emotions precipitating the attack and buy time to listen for the underlying needs that must be satisfied. Once the other party's interests are identified, we link them to our interests and needs. That way, we work together with the other party, in the spirit of mutual gain, to achieve those objectives.

In the Prisoner's Dilemma game, for example, we would have to exercise discipline, desire, and patience after turn 4 and demonstrate by our actions that we saw common goals and believed in the benefit of mutual gain. Sometimes, however, the other party perceives a series of successive cooperative responses as a sign of naïveté that invites exploitation. So, if B did not begin to collaborate, we would openly communicate while mirroring her strategy and choosing red. This would produce unacceptable results for both, creating another opportunity to communicate openly, identify shared goals, and offer the alternative of selecting black, an option producing mutual gain.

Common interests and goals were another tool used to help resolve the conflict between the CFO and the product manager. Initially, the CFO saw the product manager's objective as a request for an exception to the 15 percent reduction. The product manager saw the CFO's objective as enforcing budgetary constraints. When they both realized that their common objective was to improve the financial position of the organization, they were better able to work together to find a creative solution.

4. *Rational behavior and fair play.* Most people who desire to resolve conflict, no matter what their motivational orientation may be, expect the resolution process to be based on a *rational* dialogue between the parties that will lead to outcomes that are *fair.* Of course, individual and self-focused perceptions often cloud people's judgment about what constitutes rational behavior and fair play, and differences over these definitions are the

cause for additional, and often personal, misunderstandings. Collaboration increases, however, to the extent that each party perceives the other as acting rationally and with fairness. Likewise, collaboration is likely to decrease when one party views the other as irrational and unfair.

In general, rational behavior often is considered that which maximizes the benefits and minimizes the costs. Fairness, however, is based on the two differing notions of equity and equality. According to the principle of equity, people should receive in direct proportion to what they give. Equality, on the other hand, suggests that two parties should receive equal proportions.

Using the Prisoner's Dilemma example, when Player A selected red, Player B perceived him to be unfair (equality) and consequently shifted out of a collaborative mode. When A continued to select red, B saw A as also being irrational, thus increasing the likelihood of competition. When A selected black as a sign of good faith in turn 8, B saw him as irrational but fair, although she was not motivated to change her behavior until she saw A select black again. Then B saw A as both fair and rational, and switched (equity). By this time, however, A saw B as unfair (equality) and selected red.

Rational behavior and fair play enhance trust and willingness to seek mutual gain. Although parties may have differing perceptions, as long as each believes that the other is trying to act rationally and with fairness, then it will increase efforts to collaborate. In contrast, if one party increasingly believes that the other is acting irrationally or unfairly, then that party will become defensive and positional in an attempt at self-protection. This increases issue rigidity and ultimately efforts to compete. Efforts at collaboration will be restored as each party makes concerted efforts to communicate rationally and fairly.

The principle of mutual gain helps us create a "win-win" environment. Both parties communicate, establish common objectives, and create a variety of solutions by using rational and fair criteria and procedures. In addition, both parties work together to satisfy the needs, interests, and concerns of each individual. A focus on mutual gain ensures that we create the atmosphere of trust and understanding that leads to constructive conflict resolution.

Conclusions

The anthropologist Ruth Benedict suggested that "a synergistic institution was one that arranged it so that a person pursuing his selfish ends was automatically helping other people thereby; and that a person trying to be altruistic and helping other people and being unselfish was also automatically and willy-nilly helping along his own selfish advantages" (Maslow, 1965).

When applied, the principles of interaction create such a synergy. They take us beyond simple respect and courtesy in our interactions and toward a mutual acceptance, appreciation, and understanding, working toward mutual gain. As we help the other party, we help ourselves. As we help ourselves, we also help the other party. We realize the abundance available through an interdependent relationship that facilitates each other's growth and development as separate people. The principles of interaction keep us centered and keep us whole. They ensure that we maintain the discipline, desire, and patience to achieve constructive resolution.

4

Listening to Others

He knew the precise psychological moment when to say nothing.

Oscar Wilde

The more our knowledge increases, the more our ignorance unfolds.

John Fitzgerald Kennedy

Diane was exhausted when she finally arrived home from work. She dragged in through the door, tossed her briefcase and keys on the counter, and collapsed in the nearest chair.

"Wow, what a day!" she sighed to her husband, Peter, who was already home preparing dinner.

"Tell me about it," he said as he sliced carrots for the salad.

"You know that project I've been working on for the Improvement Committee meeting next week? Well, I've been waiting for some research from Craig for over two weeks, and today he tells me that he's not sure he'll be able to finish it in time."

"Did you find out why?"

"Yeah. He said it wasn't a top priority. Now I'm stuck trying to do it myself."

"What did he mean it wasn't a top priority?"

"Oh, I don't know. He said something about having his own workload that came first and that my research wasn't mission-critical. He is such a jerk. He doesn't know what a problem he's caused me."

"Well, you should try to convince him. Doesn't this project help his work group? You should tell him that, honey."

"I did tell him."

"Didn't he get it? Have you talked to your boss yet? I bet
your boss could talk some sense into him. Or maybe he
could sit down with Craig's boss?"

"But it's not that easy . . ."

"Sure it is, Diane. Remember when I was trying to add
the additional budget item for outside contractors and finance kept denying approval? All I had to do was line up
the opposition—with my boss, Tony from sales, and human
resources—and finance was convinced. Your boss knows
how important this is. He'll help you."

"Yeah, but you don't understand," Diane sighed.

"Sure I do, honey. Hey, don't worry, everything will work
out fine."

"Maybe." Pause. "What's for dinner?"

This type of conversation is probably familiar to all of us.
One person has a problem or an issue he or she wants to discuss.
Another person listens to the problem, offers some suggestions,
and tries to make the first person feel better.

In the above example, Peter seemed interested in Diane's
day, willing to listen, and ready to help. If asked, he would tell
us that he was trying to provide support and encouragement.
Diane, on the other hand, would tell us that Peter did not listen
and seemed to neither care about nor understand her feelings.
She might even say that he was more interested in himself and
his own accomplishments. From her perspective, she now not
only has a conflict at work to deal with, but also may have a bud-
ding conflict at home.

Confused?

Peter's error was not his intent, but his method. The problem Diane wanted to talk about was not that Craig had failed to
produce the research, but rather that she felt overwhelmed with
work and anxious about her ability to meet a deadline. However,
Peter was so quick to offer a solution that he failed to identify the
correct problem. He was so focused on persuading her to accept
his ideas that he failed to explore her real concerns, needs, and

interests. He was so motivated to provide himself with the emotional relief that comes from resolution that he failed to provide her with the satisfaction and sense of control that come from talking out her own solutions. He failed to listen to *her*.

Listening Defined

Our goal in conflict is to reach a mutually satisfactory resolution. However, the process of confronting and resolving conflict can be challenging, if not downright exasperating. We may try to build a foundation for cooperation and problem solving, and we may try to establish an effective working relationship with the other party. But early in the dispute, agendas are uncovered, uncomfortable feelings emerge, and complex issues are faced. Often, the other party does not want, or even know how, to collaborate.

It is easy to become frustrated, lose patience, and surrender our self-awareness. And as we lose sight of the collaborative objective, we become more firmly entrenched in our position and grow less detached. We try to persuade, cajole, manipulate, or dominate the other party into understanding and satisfying our needs, and we grow less concerned with understanding or satisfying the other party's needs. We stop listening, resentment builds, and the conflict becomes more personal. We feel as if we will never resolve the dispute.

But what does it mean to resolve a conflict? We can divide the word *resolve* into two parts: the prefix, *re,* and the root word, *solve. Re* means "again, back, or backward." *Solve* means "to find an answer to a problem." The whole word, *resolve,* thus can be seen as meaning "to answer the problem again" or "to go back to an answer." This implies that the solutions to a particular conflict may already exist and that the process of resolving the conflict simply brings the answers to the surface.

Listening creates an environment that allows solutions to appear. In this context, *listening* can be defined as the process of becoming aware of all the cues that another party emits. It is a process of allowing another person to communicate the conscious and subconscious, both what the other person knows and what she or he may not yet understand. It is the act of attending to what another person is saying and what he or she is not saying. Listening demands work, but it is the key to constructive conflict resolution.

Just for a moment, however, suspend the notion that you are trying to achieve a constructive, collaborative resolution. Imagine that all you really want is to deviously manipulate the other party into agreeing with your position. How do you know how to manipulate? How do you know what buttons to push to persuade the other party to help satisfy your interests? The noted American attorney Gerry Spence has said, "We cannot argue until we understand what the argument is about. Arguing into the air is analogous to the fighter who throws a hundred punches during each round and never manages to hit his opponent" (Spence, 1995). So, why listen?

- *Listening provides the information needed to resolve the conflict.* From a competitive perspective, it helps us understand how to reframe our needs so that the other party will want to satisfy them. Listening helps us understand how to tap into the other party's psyche and create the perception that we are working toward the same end. Think about the commission-driven electronics salesperson who hears that the reason you want to buy a stereo is so that you can play background music while you entertain. She will make sure to up-sell the six-CD player that will let you set the mood for an entire evening without having to interrupt conversation to change a CD. Alternatively, if you happened to be an audiophile, the same salesperson would talk to you about the technical specifications of the equipment. In either case, she was listening to you in order to satisfy her own need to earn the commission.

However, seasoned sales professionals will tell you that a manipulative approach will not be successful over the long term. They will suggest that unless you also satisfy the customer's needs, there eventually will be conflict: The customer will return the product or inform friends of the deception. Likewise, in other forms of conflict, a competitive use of listening will not achieve positive results for very long. Unless listening is a principle of interaction, based on your character and a desire to resolve the conflict, the deception will be discovered, and the intensity of the conflict will increase. Not only will you have objective issues to resolve, but you will have personal issues as well.

• *Listening reduces the impact of the personal issues of conflict.* As we have pointed out already, every conflict has objective issues and personal issues. Usually, the objective issues are easier to manage because they deal with facts, data, and information, and when we lay enough objective content on the table, people can create rational options for solving the problem. But the problem in conflict usually is not about data, but rather about the parties' perception of the data or feelings about each other. Those personal issues are much more challenging because perceptions and feelings are guided by the less rational emotional mind. And the more we try to restrain the influence of the emotional mind, the more it will wreak havoc on the rational mind and resist any effort to influence.

When we listen, however, we give the emotional mind a chance to breathe. We allow the slower rational mind to catch up and influence the perceptions generated by the rapid-firing emotional mind. Most of us would agree that when someone listens to us, we feel better. We feel as if someone is interested in us and wants to understand our ideas, thoughts, feelings, and desires. This is important because if I feel better about myself when I am with you, then I trust you and am more likely and willing to listen to your ideas. Conversely, if you demonstrate that you are not interested in me, it increases the risk that I will become defensive and competitive (especially if I have low-self-esteem to begin with). According to Ralph G. Nichols, "the most basic of all human needs is to understand and be understood" and "the best way to understand people is to listen to them" (Bentley, 1998). Thus, listening can satisfy one of our most basic human needs.

In fact, there is a strong link between listening and self-esteem. Research conducted in Japanese corporations by Akira Ikemi and Shinya Kubota indicated that employees who perceive their supervisors as having strong person-centered attitudes—a large component of which is active listening skills—exhibit less fatigue, depression, and anxiety than those who do not. They also found that this same group of employees had higher levels of motivation, better relationships with coworkers, and increased levels of productivity. In addition, their research identified that managers who participate in listening training programs are able to develop the skills and techniques that create these positive effects (Ikemi and Kubota, 1996).

However, if we want listening to be a tool for satisfying needs required to resolve conflict, it must be more than a technique or manipulative trick. Listening must be an active, voluntary process that involves recognizing, understanding, and accurately interpreting the messages received. In other words, in order to interact effectively with another person, we need to demonstrate that we understand that person. Even further, we need to demonstrate that we appreciate that person because until someone knows that we are influenced by his or her thoughts and ideas, he or she will not be open to ours. Listening creates an atmosphere that enables the other party to set aside personal issues and focus on the objective issues of the conflict. When we learn to listen actively, reflectively, and ultimately with empathy, we open the door to mutual understanding.

Learning to Communicate

Communication is one of the most important skills in life. Parents are delighted by their infant's progress from helplessness to independence, and other markers of progress, such as crawling or walking, pale in comparison to the first true words. The emergence of language is exciting because it strengthens our ability to interact with the child. It also is a reflection of what the child knows, and once a child starts using language, that knowledge increases.

Research has demonstrated that children learn a great deal about language before they ever start to talk. For example, one-day-old infants have been observed to move in tempo with the acoustic rhythms of speech. They listen for critical sound changes and can sustain such synchronized movement of several body parts for sequences of over 100 words. By the time infants are one month old, they not only can distinguish the human voice from other sounds, but also discriminate differences between sounds such as *pa* and *ba.* In addition, children prepare for the exchange of conversation by playing games such as peek-a-boo, in which one person is active and the other observes, and then the roles are reversed. Although a child's first word may not appear until she turns one or later, interaction with caregivers has already laid the groundwork for true conversation.

Children are born listeners and from a very early age seek to make sense of the conversation around them. They interpret the meaning of our communication long before they understand specific words, and they can identify emotional content such as happy, sad, angry, and worried by attending to a myriad of communication cues. Then, their own innate ability and the various processes of growth and development help them decipher the rules that will allow them to understand specific words and later produce sentences like those they hear others use. They learn, for example, that they should put an *s* on the end of the word when they mean more than one. So, "dog" becomes "dogs" and "foot" becomes "foots."

However, almost as soon as children start to talk, adults start to correct and teach. We explain that they should say "feet," not "foots," and when at age two the child asks, "Why you are doing that?" we correct her by asking, "Did you mean to say 'Why *are you* doing that?" before we answer the question. The lessons of spoken language become such a part of a child's daily ritual that by the time she begins school, she has developed a spoken language that has the structure and vocabulary of an adult's. In many cases, children under the age of six also have begun to read and write.

Early in life, children attempt to understand adult communication by making an active effort to interpret tone of voice, rate of speech, facial expressions, and other forms of nonverbal expression. However, as they learn the formal definitions, rules, and standards of language, they narrow their effort to the interpretation and application of spoken and written words. What started as a remarkable inborn ability—listening to understand emotional content and meaning—is reduced to a system of attending mostly to literal cues.

Interestingly, our teachers and role models of communication skills typically are senders, not receivers. We determine that those in authority and those we look up to do more talking than listening. Therefore, we learn that if we want to acquire control of others, our environment, and ourselves, we need to develop the verbal precision required for influence, persuasion, and domination. It is the natural path from dependent child to independent adult. In addition, higher levels of education sharpen our analytical powers and teach us how to isolate, identify, and resolve problems in a standardized and mechanical way. So when we "listen," our "listening" is most likely to become asking questions like who, what, when, where, and how. This "objective" mode of asking questions sorts out the literal message and treats events as if they were separate from the people who participated in them. It disconnects the feelings or emotions of the sender from the message the sender is communicating.

The result of our decreased listening capabilities is that we miss important cues that can help us to understand the underlying causes of our disputes. We may be intimately familiar with our own problems, but not with the mutual problems that bring us into conflict. While our experience and education develop remarkable capacities to analyze and solve problems, and then communicate the solutions persuasively, we often solve the wrong problem. Much like Peter in the story at the beginning of this chapter, we quickly diagnose the other party's condition, then offer our own advice. In other words, *we listen with the intent to respond, instead of listening with the intent to understand.*

Listening has to be more than just hearing, and more than taking in the words communicated by another person. It must attend to the whole message, which includes the deeper meaning that often goes unsaid. Listening alone will not resolve our disputes, but it will increase our effectiveness by creating an environment that allows the problems causing our conflict to be properly identified. Listening is not the answer, but when we understand how to tune into different levels of awareness, it allows solutions to materialize in our consciousness.

The Six Levels of Listening

Level 1. Passive Listening

When another person speaks, we listen at one of six levels (Figure 4-1). The first level, *passive listening,* occurs when we are silent and hear the other person talk. Our ears catch a few phrases or words now and then, or maybe not more than the humming of the speaker's voice. Our comprehension is at its lowest level. For example, suppose you are a manager who is heavily focused on reading a report when an employee, Lynn, comes to speak to you and says,

> "I've been having trouble with Sheila lately. She's in another world and has been really inconsiderate. She never cleans her work area before my shift. I had a doctor's appointment yesterday and started work thirty minutes late, only to find the place a mess. I'm sick and tired of putting up with it."

Figure 4-1. The levels of listening.

Listening Level	Listening Type	Associative Metaphor	Response Type
Level 6	Empathic	Heart	Reflective
Level 5	Active	Eyes	Reflective
Level 4	Attentive	Mind	Evaluative
Level 3	Selective	Mind	Evaluative
Level 2	Responsive	Ears	Acknowledgment
Level 1	Passive	Ears	—

As a passive listener, you might catch words such as "Sheila," "cleaning," "doctor," "late," and "sick." Your response might be that Sheila could continue cleaning and that Lynn should take the rest of the day off and get well. Passive listening has obvious problems, yet we all occasionally listen—or do not listen—at this level.

Level 2. Responsive Listening

Responsive listening is similar to passive listening except that we respond to a sender's communication with an occasional verbal encourager, such as, "Uh-huh," "Oh," or "I see." We might also nod our heads, smile, frown, or raise our eyebrows. These verbal and nonverbal *acknowledgment responses* are techniques to convey to the other person that we are paying attention and are interested. However, our responses are not coupled with actual attention. In a sense, responsive listening is pretend listening, and the use of verbal encouragers may even give the appearance of impatience with the speaker. Therefore, if you used responsive listening in the above example, it might appear to Lynn as if you were more attentive, but that you wanted her to hurry up and finish her message. Your mind would still be disengaged, and comprehension would not improve.

Level 3. Selective Listening

When we listen either passively or responsively, we listen only with our ears, our sense of hearing, but as we advance to the third level, *selective listening*, we begin to listen with our intellect. Selective listening is listening with an agenda. It is the level of listening used to argue and debate, where we listen selectively for key words or phrases that support a point we want to make. Instead of listening to the meaning conveyed by the speaker, we plan what we want to say next. When we hear something that triggers our interest or supports our case, our mind engages and we interrupt the listener with an *evaluative response*, a statement or question that suggests our thoughts or opinions. The rest of the time we are half asleep, formulating our responses, and half engaged, listening for our break-in points. Using our example, Lynn might get as far as ". . . never cleaning . . ." when you would jump in with, "That Sheila, I don't know how many times I've talked to her. Thanks for telling me about this, Lynn, I'm gonna have to fire her."

The risk of selective listening is that we may not gather enough information to know what the speaker wants or needs, and so our response or advice is based solely on *our* needs. We also risk lowering a speaker's self-esteem because *we* create and control the solution. This may inadvertently send the message that the speaker is incapable and that we have the answer to all her or his problems. This explains why our repeated efforts to help another person often only seem to make the problem worse. The person becomes increasingly dependent upon us, but also increasingly resentful of that dependence.

Level 4. Attentive Listening

Attentive listening, like selective listening, is listening with an agenda, but it is more probing, inquisitive, and analytical. Our intellect partly attends to the words and phrases that are spoken, but unlike with selective listening, we do not interrupt. Instead, we use silence, eye contact, and encouragers to concentrate on what is being said. Although we hear all of the information that is spoken, we still respond based on our own interests and needs. Attentive listening also uses evaluative responses, but in the form of leading questions, rather than statements. They serve as the primary technique to guide the information provided by the speaker and solve the problems identified by the listener. In our example, you might respond to Lynn by asking, "The place was a 'mess'?" or "What have you done about it so far, Lynn?" In the example at the beginning of the chapter, Peter used both attentive and selective listening techniques as he analyzed Diane's problem and provided advice.

When we listen attentively, we are interested in the facts and data, but not the emotional content. We are focused on solving the problems as they relate to us, not the problems that are important to the speaker. In addition to the risks of selective listening, attentive listening often looks and feels like an interrogation. In some cases, this can make a speaker shut down emotionally and stop communicating for fear of our next question.

Most of our everyday listening occurs at the first four levels. We hear, but ignore. Or we ignore, but try to appear otherwise. We analyze, evaluate, and debate. We do not mean any harm. We just cannot help it. Our brains are so active, alive, and creative that when someone else initiates a conversation, we automatically assume that that person has invited us to share all of our thoughts and ideas. This is a reaction. It is unintentionally *self-centered and self unaware*. However, little by little, the inadvertent slight and the accidental discourtesy intensify the conflicts we are trying to resolve or create conflicts where previously there were none. A deaf ear is the first sign of a closed mind.

Level 5. Active Listening

Active listening is the first level at which we suspend our own reality and attempt to understand the meaning behind the message. When we actively listen, we go outside of ourselves in search of the significant cues emitted by others. We listen with our ears to the words, but more importantly to the rate of speech, tone of voice, and linguistic patterns. We also listen with our *eyes* to the gestures, facial expressions, posture, and demeanor. We listen to the sounds and the silence, and we stay open to receiving the sender's subconscious messages.

In active listening, the listener uses *reflective responses* to provide feedback to the sender. He or she may restate or rephrase the words, or reflect the mood identified by the nonverbal cues. The reflective response is used to verify that the listener understands the meaning of the communication and to encourage the speaker to keep talking. This creates an atmosphere of acceptance and understanding in which the sender is empowered to explore the problem and determine her or his own solutions. For example, you might respond to Lynn by saying, "It sounds as if you are frustrated when Sheila doesn't clean up because you may be left with more work to do." You reflected back the mood, "frustrated," and you restated in your words what Lynn said, "Sheila doesn't clean up," and what she implied, "may be left with more work to do."

When we respond reflectively, we are really asking, "Here is what I heard you say. Did I understand you correctly?" The sender is able to keep control of the conversation by confirming that we understand or by providing more information to help us comprehend. When the sender understands that we understand, he or she gains confidence in our listening ability and, as a result, shares more information. Even if we did not "get it," we still boost the sender's self-esteem by implying that we need his or her help in order to understand.

The downside to active listening is that it is still mostly technique. We may understand the words of the other person, but only intellectually and at arm's length. We may accept that this person has particular feelings, but we still may not accept that these feelings are *justified from that person's perspective,* an important part of acceptance. The active listening environment allows us to accept the message, but we do not have to understand or accept the messenger.

Level 6. Empathic Listening

The highest level of listening, *empathic listening,* is listening with the intent to accept and understand the other person's frame of reference. It is total suspension of your reality and total immersion in the other person's reality. This does not mean that we suspend detached responsibility and become the other person, but rather that we attend to that person's feelings "as if" we were that person (L. G. Wispe, 1968). We incorporate the principles of interaction so we can see the world the way she or he sees the world. Empathic listening is listening with the ears, mind, eyes, and *heart* to become aware of the sender's feelings and emotions. It requires acceptance of the person. As Carl Rogers (1961) stated in his work on total listening:

> I also find the relationship is significant to the extent that I feel a continuing desire to understand—a sensibive empathy with each of the client's feelings and communications as they seem to him at that moment. Acceptance does not mean much until it involves understanding. It is only as I understand the feelings and thoughts which seem so horrible to you, or so weak, or so sentimental, or so bizarre—it is only as I see them as you see them, and accept them and you, that you feel

really free to explore all the hidden nooks and frightening crannies of your inner and often buried experience.

Rogers implies that empathic listening is not an additional active listening technique, but rather a change in attitude—a principle of interaction. It requires that you separate the person from the problem in the conflict and accept the person as valuable and likable. In fact, research has demonstrated that liking another person greatly increases sensitivity toward that person. Eisman and Levy (1960), for example, showed that lip reading was more accurate the more the reader liked the communicator, while Suchman (1956) discovered that people who were more favorable toward others were more accurate in estimating the feelings of others. In other words, liking the person enhances our capacity for empathy and understanding.

The Role of Empathy

Empathy is the ability to know how another person feels, or the ability to "walk in someone else's shoes." It goes beyond an ability to understand the situation of another. It is "the inner experience of sharing in and comprehending the momentary psychological state of another person" (Schafer, 1959). Empathy is the ability to "feel" for the situation of others.

Countless studies have demonstrated the importance of empathy in developing and sustaining our interpersonal relationships. Conversely, the absence of empathy, in the extreme, is an indicator of a variety of psychological disorders and is frequently observed in criminal psychopaths. Individuals who demonstrate the affective aspects of empathy have lower stress levels and are better adjusted emotionally. They also are more outgoing, more popular, and more sensitive, and, not surprisingly, have better romantic lives (Rosenthal, 1977). A number of studies have found that a manager's ability to empathize can significantly affect the behavior and attitudes of that manager's subordinates. These studies have indicated that self-awareness, self-exploration, therapeutic success, and satisfaction are enhanced in those individuals exposed to empathic superiors (Egan, 1975; Gladstein, 1977).

As a result, empathy is considered one of the crucial ingredients not only for maintaining one's own psychological health, but also for affecting the emotional health of others.

Developmental psychologists suggest that humans demonstrate empathy almost from birth. For example, in early infancy, children attend to and are stimulated by the strong behaviors of others in their environment. They laugh when others laugh, and cry when others cry (Simner, 1971). This may result from conditioning, in which cues of pain or displeasure from another person become associated with the child's own past experiences of pain (Levine and Hoffman, 1975). This occurs long before children are able to have any cognitive appreciation for the existence of themselves apart from others. As children reach their first birthday, they start to realize that the sadness is not theirs and, while they still may cry, demonstrate helping and comforting behavior. And by the time they are two and a-half years old, they are sufficiently aware of the other person as a separate being and know enough to bring a teddy bear to a sobbing brother or sister.

Empathy is thought to develop in much the same way as cognition and moral maturity, and its highest level, referred to as *developmental empathy* by Robert Emde (1989), requires the cognitive component of "perspective taking." Perspective taking reflects an ability to shift perspectives—to step outside the self—when dealing with other people. Children are thought to progress from a self-oriented personal distress reaction to a rudimentary other-oriented, perspective-taking mode. More sophisticated aspects of empathy, however, may develop at different rates. In fact, some studies suggest that readiness for empathy learning may not fully develop until early adulthood, and that not all adults learn the actual skills required to empathize. Therefore, while adults maintain the capacity to learn higher levels of empathy, it typically is not fully exercised. The skills of empathy are crucial, however, if an individual expects to learn how to listen and communicate empathically (Davis and Franzoi, 1991).

Empathic listening requires the development of three primary characteristics of empathy (Heilman, 1972). First, we must have the ability to accurately perceive the *content* of the communication from another person, the meaning of the spoken words.

Second, we must attend to the *emotional core*. In other words, we must understand the unexpressed meanings of the message. Third, we must be able to adopt an *"as if"* quality, meaning that we attend to the other person's feelings *"as if"* those feelings were our own. We must sense the other person's anger, fear, or confusion as if it were our own, but remain detached responsibly, without our own anger, fear, or confusion becoming intertwined. These three attributes allow us to move from a rational understanding of the speaker to emotional acceptance.

Empathic listening requires more than simply saying, "I understand." It requires that we convey understanding of both the content and the emotion of the speaker's explicit message, and that we reflect understanding of the implicit, or unspoken and implied, core. For example, suppose a coworker were to say,

"I may just quit this job. I'm tired of always having more to do than I can handle."

Our response to the explicit message would be,

"You seem frustrated because you have so much work to do."

Our response to the implicit message would be,

"It sounds as if you are feeling overwhelmed right now. It gets you down and maybe makes you feel unappreciated."

The response to the explicit message tried to convey understanding of the speaker's stated message, the meaning behind what was said. However, the response to the implicit message went further, trying to convey understanding of what was expressed emotionally. The speaker may not be conscious of the emotions expressed by her nonverbal behavior, but by responding in the "as if" mode, we let her know what we saw and felt as she was communicating. We are not trying to tell the speaker what she is feeling, only to disclose our emotional understanding.

Empathy cannot be established without the ability to develop close interpersonal relationships, even with people we have never met, or with whom we have little in common. Establishing a "close interpersonal relationship" does not mean that we become lifelong pals. Rather, it implies that we are sincerely interested in and accepting of the person as a person.

An inability or unwillingness to develop these empathic relationships can have a noticeable impact on our daily interactions. For example, during an exit interview, a human resources manager for a *Fortune* 500 company asked a longtime employee why she was quitting after twenty-four years. The employee, Rhonda, who had not yet found another job, was quitting one year before she became eligible for early retirement. She responded by saying,

> "When I first started working for this company, it was like a family. We all got along and even did things after work together. My boss and his wife even had us over to his house for supper now and then. But over the last several years, things have changed. I rarely even see my new boss. He's in meetings all the time, and when he isn't, he doesn't come out of his office except to give me another assignment. My first few bosses knew that I bowled on Tuesday nights, that I sang in my church choir, what sports my boys played, and that I liked a good game of bridge. This new fellow doesn't even know my birthday. In fact, I'm pretty sure he doesn't know that my husband had a heart attack three months ago—at least he's never said anything about it. How can I work for someone who doesn't want to know a thing about me?"

We all desire close interpersonal relationships with others. They make us feel accepted and a part of something bigger than ourselves. However, such intimacy is not encouraged, or even accepted, in the majority of the relationships we encounter throughout life, especially in the workplace. Moreover, as in Rhonda's case, a manager's inability to establish a relationship can be a contributing factor to increased alienation and lower self-acceptance and self-esteem. Without even a superficial relationship, Rhonda's manager was not able to maintain the continued interaction required to demonstrate basic understanding.

Empathic understanding, however, carries with it a risk. If we open ourselves up to deeply understanding another person, we risk being influenced by that person. One reason managers often do not establish close interpersonal relationships with their subordinates is that it makes delivering difficult information more challenging. These managers are afraid that if they had to fire an employee, a personal relationship would cause them to cave in and accommodate continued poor performance. The opposite is, in fact, true. Empathy helps us fire employees with caring. It helps us manage and resolve the personal issues by demonstrating caring and understanding. The empathic relationship creates an environment that helps the other person separate the personal issues from the objective issues in the conflict and accept the decision as fair and objective.

Our empathic understanding of other people opens them up to understanding us. If we enter a conflict positionally, with only the desire to make our point, then we will never have a collaborative resolution. We may win in the short term, but long-term resolution will prove difficult. We have to be influenced in order to influence. We have to broaden our perceptions if we want to broaden the perceptions of others. Empathy helps us to listen without feeling defensive and to recognize that divergent perceptions often hold the key to resolution.

Obstacles to Effective Listening

While empathic listening often takes time and effort, correcting misunderstandings and confronting the results of not initially creating the right environment takes more time. Once trust is lost, it is hard to regain, and once you are perceived as insincere or uncaring, it is difficult for others to change their perception.

As you improve your listening skills, the process does not take as much time as you think. You quickly will develop a deep understanding of the other person and be able to convey that understanding. Such understanding makes it easy for others to peel away their layers of defensiveness and display the core of themselves, where the problem really lives and where personal issues are clouding the objective issues.

Unfortunately, we listen with only 25 percent efficiency, although we spend at least 45 to 60 percent of our communication time listening. In fact, fewer than 15 percent of all individuals rate themselves as better than average listeners (Steil, 1980). In a recent survey of 443 companies in Canada and the United States conducted by Olsten Corporation, a temporary-help firm based in New York City, 74 percent said that significant improvement was needed in the listening skills of their managers and employees.

Before we discuss the techniques of good listening, however, it might be helpful to review some of the obstacles that prevent effective listening. These errors can be broken down into three categories: internal, external, and response.

Internal Errors

1. *Internal preoccupation.* Normal speech occurs at 125 to 250 words per minute, but effective listening can occur at a rate of 500 words per minute. Consequently, since we think faster than a speaker can speak, the brain uses that surplus time for other things. We may begin to evaluate the speaker or look for hidden motives. We may also begin to think of abstract questions to ask or points we want to make. We make our to-do lists, think about what we want for dinner, or travel to our mental Tahiti.

Part of the challenge of listening is learning to attend to other elements of the message and messenger. It is learning to use the 250- to 375-word-per-minute capacity to receive important nonverbal cues that will help us go beyond literal content to understand the intent and deeper meaning.

2. *Self-involvement.* Self-involvement occurs when we are preoccupied with our own relationship to the interaction, rather than giving ourselves fully to the topic of conversation. We may start to listen, but our mind drifts back to prior points, considers items of unrelated concern, or wonders how we "appear" to the speaker. Various thoughts run through our mind, such as, "I hope I can help" or "Does he think I'm capable?" or "Is my hair

okay?" or "I remember a time when . . ." We try to appear engaged and interested, but our eyes glaze over as we ponder the self-relevance of what is said.

Self involvement also occurs when the content of a message hits a hot zone. If the content is sufficiently anxiety-arousing, we may become overly conscious of our own emotional state and attend to our feelings about the message rather than the actual content or meaning. Instead of becoming preoccupied and losing focus, however, the aroused hot zone should serve as a cue to listen more attentively.

3. *Selective attention.* Sometimes speakers repeat messages that we have heard before in other contexts. The information does not appear new or distinct, and we assume that we know what the speaker is going to say next. Consequently, we put the speaker into one category or another, and stop attending to both content and meaning. We also listen only to the sections that are relevant to our needs and interests. When a topic returns to something unrelated to our needs, we toss the information into a previously formed category.

4. *Listening with an agenda.* We listen for facts that will prove our point. We listen to criticize the sender or the message. We also tend to be so focused on our own opinions that we interpret others' messages so that they agree with our ideas. Listening with an agenda is judgmental, evaluative, and analytical. It ignores important emotional cues that give us additional information required to resolve our disputes.

External Errors

1. *External distraction.* Background noise, uncomfortable seating, or visual distractions capture our attention and interfere with our listening. The telephone rings, our pager beeps, or we notice the "to-do" list sitting on our desk. We disregard the speaker and give our main concern to something unconnected with the interaction. This usually is a sign that we are not as interested in the message as we are in our own concerns and needs. We have too much going on to listen effectively, and we

subconsciously seek an "out." In other words, we are distracted because we want to be distracted.

2. *Communicator style.* Poor listeners often focus on speaker idiosyncrasies to the detriment of retention. Communicator difficulties such as accents, verbal "twitches," excessive gesturing, and repeated expressions often are more salient than the message. Sometimes the length of the speaker's remarks or the clothes that the speaker is wearing can be equally distracting. The average listener tends to mentally correct, abbreviate, or belittle these personal quirks and fails to assimilate the real meaning of the message.

We can also be significantly influenced by the *halo effect* in that one or more of a sender's salient features can influence our overall judgment of the message. For example, if a communicator is perceived to be attractive, we are more likely to also portray that person as more intelligent and likable. Thus, our first impression of features that have nothing to do with the message influence our ability to interpret accurately. Both positive and negative traits may contribute a halo effect.

3. *Preconceptions.* We all tend to be influenced by past interactions with the sender. If the relationship has been strained, it is often difficult to move beyond our memory of the previous dispute. Instead of listening to the present communication, we recall earlier feelings or issues, and relate those elements to the current message. Consequently, we may misinterpret information or ascribe more significance to it than is justified.

In addition, research has demonstrated that preconceptions can significantly influence the short-term outcome of an interaction. If someone tells us that we will have a positive conversation with a specific individual, we are more likely to perceive the interaction favorably, even if the results would indicate otherwise. A biased preconception is likely to affect our perception of both the content and the meaning of the message.

4. *Constituencies.* The influence of third parties and cultural filters can alter how we translate the content of a sender's message. A third party can set our expectations or interfere with the conversation, and our cultural filters can cause us to misinterpret the meaning of verbal and nonverbal cues. We are likely to

use our ethnocentric frame of reference to help us make sense of information we do not understand. Although this can help us toward an improved comprehension, overreliance on in-group definitions prevents true empathic understanding.

Response Errors

1. *Discount.* Discounting is the act of accidentally minimizing the importance of another person's comments. For example, picture a friend saying, "I'm not going to try to finish my degree. I've been out of school too long to try to go back now." If we respond by saying, "Ah, don't worry. You'll do just fine," we are discounting.

Our intent is to provide support and encouragement because, after all, we may have more confidence in the person's ability than he or she does. However, when we discount, we risk accidentally sending a different message. Our response might be interpreted as, "You are foolish and stupid because you worry over such trivial matters." If our friend really did have concerns he wanted to discuss with us, we just told him that we were not interested in talking about them.

A discounting statement indicates that we are listening from our own perspective, without detached responsibility, and have become focused more on our own needs than on the needs of the sender. In effect, we are trying to resolve the discomfort *we* feel because of the sender's concern. The discounting response says, "I feel uncomfortable because you feel uncomfortable, and if I can minimize your pain, then I will feel better." The discounting response brings resolution to our part of the conflict, but shuts down the emotional expression of the sender. Some examples of discounting responses are:

"Don't let it get to you . . ."

"You don't mean that . . ."

"Don't worry . . ."

"You'll be just fine . . ."

"What's the big deal . . ."

"It's okay . . ."

2. *Advise.* The second common response error is advising. Much like Peter from the beginning of the chapter, when we advise, we offer our own suggestions and ideas for solving the problem. Unfortunately, we are solving the problems that *we* identify, not necessarily the problem the sender needs to resolve. We are prescribing without first diagnosing the problem. If our friend expressed his concern about going back to school, some advising responses might be, "You just need to budget your time and study," or "Maybe you could get a tutor," or "You really need to have a degree if you want to progress in your career." In all these cases, we have assumed that we know what the sender wants to resolve, when in fact, he may not need resolution at all. He may simply want to talk to someone about his feelings and relieve built-up emotional pressure. Once he gets it off his chest, he may feel better, and the conflict may be gone.

Another risk associated with advising is that we take control away from the sender and solve the problem too soon. Even if we have correctly identified the problem the sender wants to solve, it is important to remember that *she* wants to solve the problem. When we offer solutions, we may unintentionally send the message that the sender is incapable of solving the problem on her own. We also might provide the solutions before the sender has had a chance to think through her own solutions. She may not be ready to hear solutions, no matter how correct and valuable ours may be, because her emotional mind is still preventing her rational mind from accepting data. Until she has gained control of her emotional mind, advice will be misinterpreted, misperceived, and misunderstood. Our role in the empathic listening mode is not to solve the problem, but to help the sender get ready to solve the problem on her or his own.

3. *Derail.* When we derail, we take the conversation off track and in a direction different from what the speaker intended. The derail response to our friend with fears about finishing school might be, "I know, I've been out of school for fifteen years. Gosh,

I can't believe it's been that long . . ." or "I would have a hard time going back myself because . . ." or "Did you hear that Sandy is going back to school?"

A derailing response communicates *our* thoughts and interests, and ignores the concerns expressed by the sender. Derailing is self-centered responding that tells the speaker that he is not important, and accidentally initiates a new personal issue in the conflict. In addition, our digression makes the speaker lose his train of thought and delays the resolution process. The derail response is a form of avoidance because it postpones discussion of the real issues.

4. *Analyze.* We are analyzing when we probe, interpret, judge, and evaluate the sender's remarks, providing feedback in the form of questions and statements. For example, analytical responses to our friend might be, "Why do you think that?" or "How long have you been out of school?" or "It sounds like you're just looking for an excuse not to go back to college."

When we analyze, we are really trying to uncover the information that will help *us* resolve the speaker's problem. Sure, our intention is to help the sender, but our questions often make her feel that she is being interrogated, or pushed toward revealing things that are not of interest to her. The sender may also feel that we are trying to show off and play amateur psychologist. She has come to us to discuss *her* problem in *her* way, but we make it *our* conversation by analyzing her remarks from *our* perspective. Much like discounting, advising, and derailing, analyzing is self-centered responding that shows that we are not listening.

How to Listen

Empathic listening requires more than technique, it requires the right intentions. On the other hand, sometimes our good intentions are misinterpreted because of poor technique. That is, we may try to apply the principles of interaction and listen empathically, but something we do or say gives the other party the impression that we are attempting to discount, advise, derail, or analyze. For some reason, the other person does not believe that we have his or her best interests in mind.

In general, trying to listen empathically is better than not trying at all. Most often the other party will sense your intentions and give you the benefit of the doubt. However, proper technique will greatly enhance your chances for success. Mastering the skills of empathic listening ensures that others receive the right signals from you. It also ensures that you maintain your focus and overcome the obstacles to effective listening.

The technique of empathic listening has four steps. The listener must:

1. Attend to both content and emotion.
2. Suspend judgment and analysis.
3. Convey understanding of the explicit and implicit message.
4. Remain sensitive to signs of resistance and defensiveness.

Attend to Both Content and Emotion

The first step of empathic listening involves attending to the sender's verbal and nonverbal cues. This requires that you clear the decks and remove all distractions from your environment. Treat listening as a challenging mental task that requires your full attention and concentration. When you are at the office, put away your work, forward your calls, turn off the computer, and close your door. When you are at home, stop what you are doing, turn off the television and radio, and sit down in a quiet and comfortable room. If you are in the middle of something important or for some other reason cannot give the sender your full attention, let him or her know that by saying, "What you have to say is important to me, and I really want to listen to you [or discuss this with you, or give you my full attention]. However, I'm in the middle of [let the sender know what you are doing]. Can we schedule a time later when I can give you my full attention?" Set a time and follow through. This sends the message that the person is important and you want to dedicate time just for him or her.

Next, look at the other person. This may seem like an obvious point, but it is vitally important. Eye contact demonstrates interest and attention, and lets the sender know that you are still engaged in the interaction. Do not stare, but look into the person's eyes and face to show your respect and concern. Stay relaxed and use a neutral body posture that presents acceptance. (Note: Direct eye contact is preferred throughout most of the world. However, in some Latin American and Asian cultures, it is considered respectful to look down when interacting with someone in a position of authority.)

Now that environmental distractions have been set aside and you are sending attentive nonverbal signals, begin to listen to the sender. Attend to the words to understand the content, and attend to the nonverbals to understand the feeling behind the content. Listen for the overall substance of what the person is saying. Listen to the tone of voice, the rate of speech, and the inflection. Listen for subtle changes, such as the words that are emphasized and the parts of the message that appear important. Attend to what the person is saying and not saying. Watch the body language. What do the person's facial expressions convey? When do the person's eyes shift? When does the person change his or her posture?

All of these signals may give you clues to the thoughts and emotions underlying the message. The nonverbals may indicate comfort or discomfort with a particular element of the communication. Also, both words and gestures may serve as trial balloons sent up to determine whether it is safe to let you in on deeper thoughts, feelings, and needs.

As you listen, resist the temptation to interrupt, finish the speaker's sentences, or draw conclusions. Do not plan what you want to say next, or intrude physically or verbally. Be in the moment and take in the full sense of the message. Be present in hearing, mind, heart, and spirit with the other person. Let the person ramble and digress. Let her or him be silent.

Suspend Judgment and Analysis

Throughout the process of listening, it is important that you defer evaluating the message and the messenger. This is clearly one of the more difficult aspects of listening empathically. It requires maintaining self-awareness and following the principles of interaction. We cannot let our memories, experience, or doubts about the sender interfere with our ability to listen to him or her. We also must suspend our expertise and resist our desire to offer advice, admonitions, or counsel. We have to let the other person come to his or her own conclusions, and we have to trust the person's ability to handle his or her own emotions, work through the issues, and find solutions to his or her own problems.

It is important that we remember to maintain detached responsibility. This does not mean that we ignore our feelings—in fact, quite the opposite. We should attend to our feelings and stay aware of how the message is affecting our emotions. This self-awareness will help prevent our emotions from becoming intermingled with the other person's message. When we become emotionally involved—whether to judge, evaluate, or react—we tend to hear what we want to hear, not what is actually said.

Inevitably, another person will say something that will stir an emotional reaction within us. Be self-aware; do not react. You do not always have to agree with the speaker, but you always must agree that if you were in the speaker's shoes, you might see it the same way. If we become too emotionally involved, we may need to ask for a break, or time-out, to regain our self-control. Demonstrate acceptance by saying, "I really appreciate your sharing your thoughts with me, and I have a lot to consider. Could I have a few moments to think about what you have told me?"

Convey Understanding of the Explicit and Implicit Message

Step 3 in the empathic listening process is where technique is most important. How we convey understanding can either open inner doors of trust, awareness, and expression or close and lock all portals to insight. A reflective response that expresses empathy creates the sense of peace that individuals need in order to release pent-up emotions, explore their feelings, and feel accepted and understood.

The wording of the reflective response can lead to different levels of effectiveness in our interactions and can have a short-term impact on the emotional bond established between listener and speaker. Reflective responses that are *neutral* or that imply an *alternative possibility*, for example, tend to produce emotional responses of lower intensity than statements that imply that the speaker's interpretation is correct (Nugent and Halvorson, 1995). A neutral response will help us indicate acceptance of the person, without also communicating agreement with the person's behavior. In addition, statements that are directive, guiding, or closed-ended are ineffective if personal issues are more important to the speaker than objective issues (Nagel, Hoffman, and Hill, 1995). We need to remain neutral and let speakers "clear out" the personal issues at their pace, rather than influencing them to get down to business too soon.

There are five different levels of reflective response that take us from active listening to empathic listening (Figure 4-2). All of them may be effective at different times, but empathic responses convey much greater interest and understanding.

The first level is to *repeat* the content. We restate what the person said to us word for word. For example, suppose a friend, Tina, says,

> "I can't believe I have to do this stupid presentation on Wednesday. I should have known I'd get stuck with it."

> *Repeat:* "You can't believe you have to do the presentation on Wednesday. You believe you should have known you'd get stuck with it."

Figure 4-2. Reflective responses.

	Type of Listening
Repeat the content	Active
Rephrase the content	Active
Reflect the **E**xplicit feeling	Empathic
Reflect the **I**mplicit feeling	Empathic
Rephrase and **R**eflect	Empathic

We have essentially repeated what Tina said and demonstrated that we were paying attention. We have not discounted, advised, derailed, or analyzed, and Tina knows that we have heard the content of her communication (with our ears). However, notice that by including "believe" in the second sentence, we implied the existence of an alternative interpretation. This is one way of staying in the "as if" mode and conveying understanding while maintaining detached responsibility. Had we said, "You should have known you'd get stuck with it," we might have implied that Tina was correct in her assumption. If Tina was uncertain whether she should have known and was looking to us for validation of the contrary, we may have just insulted her, adding to the conflict.

The second-level response is to *rephrase* the content. We paraphrase or summarize what we hear. In this case, our response to Tina would be,

> *Rephrase:* "You can't believe you got stuck having to do the presentation."

By using the rephrase response, we have demonstrated an additional level of understanding because we were able to restate the content in our own words. Nevertheless, we still have not conveyed understanding of the emotional core. As we shift from an intellectual understanding to an emotional understanding, we will see a remarkable difference in the affective state of the speaker.

The third-level response is where we first begin to show empathy when we *reflect the explicit* feeling.

> *Reflect^e :* "You sound frustrated."

When we reflect the explicit feeling, we try to convey our understanding of the meaning behind the stated message. Tina is feeling frustrated on the surface, her conscious level of emotional awareness. By confirming that we see her frustration, we give her another boost of energy to talk through the problem. Had we made any of the response errors, we would have risked zapping her energy and shutting down her desire to resolve the conflict.

At the fourth level, we *reflect the implicit* emotion, or the deeper, possibly unconscious level of emotion.

> *Reflect*: "It sounds as if you are feeling overwhelmed and a little uneasy."

When we reflect the implicit, we need to pay special attention to the nonverbal cues. Depending on the signals, Tina may have implied that she was feeling uneasy, unappreciated, singled out, or set up. It is important to get a sense of her true implicit emotion before reflecting implicitly because we risk putting her on the defensive.

Important: Empathic listening is not effective when it is only technique. If you do not feel the implied emotion, do not try to search for it. Instead, reflect the explicit feeling.

The final level of reflective response is a combination of rephrasing the content and reflecting the feeling. We can use either the explicit or the implicit reflecting response.

> *Rephrase and reflect:* "It sounds as if you are feeling overwhelmed right now and a little uneasy about having to do the presentation on Wednesday."

We almost can hear Tina say mentally, "Yeah! That is exactly how I am feeling, and you are the first person who seems to understand me. I am so glad I came to talk to you."

At this point, people will probably go a little deeper and reveal more to us that will help us understand their real needs and interests. Most likely, their first statement was the front-page headline to the story buried on page twenty-seven of their mental newspaper. We have to let them read the story and turn the pages to reveal the rest of the story—at their own pace. The reflective response encourages them to keep up the effort to help us understand.

When they feel we understand them, they will want to understand us. This is the remarkable turning point in conflict. The other party starts to ask us for our thoughts, advice, information, and opinions. Only after we have demonstrated acceptance and empathy will they trust that we are working toward mutual gain.

Remain Sensitive to Signs of Resistance and Defensiveness

The final step in the empathic listening process is to stay aware of the other person's reaction to our reflective responses. When people feel defensive, barriers go up and communication breaks down. Resistance and defensiveness are natural reactions when people feel hurt, embarrassed, backed into the corner, or out of control. Our job when listening is to help communicators regain their sense of self-esteem and confidence. We want them to feel in charge of the interaction.

Attend to the other party's response to what you have said. If she feels she has been heard, she will nod, say, "uh-huh," and continue to talk in an informative or revealing tone. If you have not reflected accurately and she does not feel understood, she will let you know. She may correct you and suggest an alternative feeling, or she may shut down all communication and exhibit closed body language, such as furrowed brows, pursed lips, crossed arms, or bowed head. She may sound more aggressive or go on the attack. She also may start to rationalize and offer lengthy explanations of why your perception is wrong. Her statements may become emotionally charged, or she may deny that a problem exists. Whatever the particular defensive signal may be, it will tell you to return to step 1 of the empathic listening process and begin to attend more closely.

Effective listening is not just listening with the ears. It is listening with the eyes and heart. Skilled listeners can watch a communicator on a video with the sound turned down and reflect the explicit and implicit messages with remarkable accuracy. Emotional meaning is revealed through the nonverbals.

When you run out of time, patience, or energy for the interaction, let the other person know. Stop responding. Trying to fake empathic listening is not consistent with the principles of interaction and inevitably undermines your credibility and the other person's sense of trust. Preventing resistance and defensiveness in the communicator as well as in ourselves will maintain constructive interaction.

When to Use Empathic Listening

The active or empathic listening mode is not always the best choice. In many instances, it would be inappropriate to the interaction. For example, when we are shooting the breeze with a friend or making small talk in the supermarket, the expectation is not to be understood, but to connect. It might be better in these cases to exchange pleasantries and information without seeking to deeply understand. Sometimes others want us to engage in verbal sparring or more directive forms of communication.

On the other hand, empathic listening is an effective default mode of listening. It keeps us on our toes and makes us more aware of others in our environment. Until you have information that indicates otherwise, stay in that mode. As the other party invites your opinions, thoughts, advice, and banter, share them. However, share them with the purpose of reciprocal self-disclosure. In other words, reveal yourself as a tool to understand more about the other party.

We should always use empathic listening during the early stages of conflict, especially if the relationship is strained or trust is low. It is important when we want, or need, to understand the other person's perspective. If personal issues are invading the conflict and tensions seem high, empathic listening will help separate the personal from the objective and reduce the intensity of the interaction. Very often, this is simply the result of letting the other person vent, but the results seem to be enhanced when we identify the explicit or implicit feeling the person is conveying.

Active listening and empathic listening are practical tools for the workplace because they help us understand details that often go overlooked. These modes are useful when the information is unfamiliar, complex, or important. These listening skills also help us identify with and include those who often feel disenfranchised. By using these skills, we can bring their ideas to the surface and include them in our decision-making processes.

Conclusions

The variety of issues and influencing factors inherent in conflict create inevitable misunderstandings between people. Our instinctive reaction to this confusion is to try harder to be understood. Employees gather more data, departments perform more analysis, and organizations spend more to promote product features and benefits. In more personal relationships, we yell, scream, criticize, defend, and attack as well as color our hair, listen to different music, have affairs, and get divorced. Our actions shout for attention, and when no one listens, we try to create independent solutions to our perceptions of the conflict.

Most people and organizations do not take the necessary time and effort to listen to the conflict. Instead, we react by analyzing the superficial problem and quickly offering our own solutions. We listen with the intent to respond, instead of with the intent to understand, and in the process, we create additional disagreement.

Listening breaks this cycle of destructive conflict. It is supportive communication, based on acceptance and a desire to learn how to create the interdependent solutions required for mutual gain. Carl Rogers once said, "The more I am open to the realities in me and in the other person, the less do I find myself wishing to rush in to 'fix things.'" As we listen to other people with greater depth, we become more accepting of their needs, and of our own. We facilitate a relationship that helps us understand their interests and explore the options for constructive, collaborative resolution.

5

Resolving Conflict

The devils enter uninvited when the house stands empty.
For other kinds of guests, you have first to open the door.

Dag Hammarskjöld, *Markings*

There is a generally accepted notion that it takes only one to start a fight, but it takes two to stop it. One person, group, or nation decides unilaterally that it is dissatisfied with a particular issue, confronts its adversary, and forces that adversary into battle to determine the final settlement.

We have seen this portrayed countless times: The "bad guy" rides into town, pushes open the saloon doors, walks menacingly over to a cowboy who is playing a peaceful game of cards, and says, "Meet me at high noon." Of course, the cowboy, who is a silent man who never hurt anyone, must defend his honor, pride, and reputation. So, he goes out at noon and, as onlookers gather in fear and trepidation, walks out to the center of town to meet his fate. With hands resting on their six-shooters, they stare each other down. The bad guy says, "Draw." Guns fire, the crowd gasps, and after the dust settles, our Hero rides off into the sunset, back to his humble ranch. Once again, the righteous prevail.

The assumption is that the cowboy did nothing to provoke the bad guy, and that the bad guy's grievances are unjust and without merit. In reality, the cowboy probably took the bad guy's land in a questionable real estate deal or shot the bad guy's brother for trespassing. Therefore, while one person initiated the fight, the conflict did begin for real reasons on both sides. The apparent unilateral conflict was really a bilateral conflict in disguise.

It appears that the assumption of the unilateral emergence of conflict is false. The assumption that ending the conflict requires two may be equally false. If one party exercises the principles of interaction, listens, and uses the six steps of collaborative resolution, that party may be able to end the conflict constructively. At the very least, he or she may be able to prevent the conflict from turning into a fight by choosing an alternative to destructive interaction. While cowboys may still choose to have a gun battle, in most other situations one person can change the game of competition into a game of collaboration that seeks mutual gain.

There is a difference between resolving a conflict and managing a conflict. Resolving a conflict ends the dispute by satisfying the interests of both parties. Managing a conflict contains specialized interaction that prevents a dispute from becoming a destructive battle. Managing a conflict attends to the personal issues so as to allow for a constructive relationship, even though the objective issues may not be resolvable. For example, the former Soviet Union and the United States managed their conflict during the Cold War by using a variety of mechanisms. The objective issues in the dispute were not resolved, and neither were the personal issues, which contained significant perceptual differences. However, both sides attended significantly to the relationship to keep the disagreement from turning into a destructive battle.

Our goal in conflict *always* should be to seek a resolution based on mutual gain. Realistically, however, resolution is not always possible. When this is the case, we must manage the conflict to ensure that the relationship is constructive and that open communication is maintained. We Listen to Conflict to understand the other party and demonstrate the acceptance required to maintain the relationship.

The Framework for Conflict Resolution

Conflict can be managed in a variety of ways. Using the dual-concerns model discussed in Chapter 1, the method we choose to manage the conflict will depend upon the relationship between the concern we have for *our own needs* and the concern we have for *the other party's needs*. It also will be determined by the situational variables that affect the interaction.

When conflicts arise, we assess a variety of factors before selecting our approach to the situation. We may choose to *compete*, or dominate, where we try to impose our will on the other side through physical or psychological means, or we may choose to *accommodate*, or surrender, and cede victory to the other side. Likewise, we may decide to *withdraw* by either doing nothing or refusing to participate in the conflict altogether, or we may *collaborate* and reach a constructive and mutually acceptable solution. And if none of those approaches proves effective, we might choose third-party intervention, a form of collaboration in which an individual or group external to the conflict intercedes to move both parties toward agreement. (We will talk more about third-party intervention in Chapter 6.)

While each of the above orientations represents a way to manage conflict, only two—collaboration and third-party intervention—are, by definition, focused on mutual gain and resolution. These two approaches consider the interests of both parties and are most likely to use empathic listening as the primary tool to enhance understanding. The other methods deal unilaterally with the conflict and fail to manage the interdependence of the dispute.

In order to understand the mechanisms behind the four orientations to conflict, it is useful to examine how these orientations can be applied. The study of negotiation, one form of conflict resolution, provides two opposite approaches for dealing with disputes. Most often, we think of negotiation in the formal sense seen in the business or diplomatic environment, where two or more parties bargain to reach agreement. However, two types of negotiation, *competitive bargaining* and *collaboration*, also provide good models for understanding different ways of resolving our conflicts.

Competitive Bargaining

When most people think of negotiation, they think of *competitive bargaining*. In this type of negotiation, a seller asks for more than he expects and a buyer offers less than she is willing to pay. Then, through a series of concessions, the two sides meet somewhere in the middle where each side is reasonably satisfied. This form of negotiation also is frequently called *distributive bargaining* or *concession-convergence*. It maintains a competitive, win-lose orientation, with the goals of one party and the attainment of those goals in direct conflict with the goals of the other party. In other words, competitive bargaining is a positional conflict in which "winning" is determined by how much of the original position was obtained. The parties believe that resources are fixed and limited, and that they must battle to maximize their share of the wealth.

In competitive bargaining, each party uses strategy, tactics, and tricks to achieve its objective, and whether one of both parties will achieve their goal depends upon their ability to "play the game." Each party seeks to extract information from the other party that will help in identifying appropriate counteroffers, while revealing as little accurate information as possible about its own preferences. The final agreement often depends on the willingness of one party to stake out a tough and extreme position that causes the other party to make concessions. Labor-management disputes and international negotiations often use this model of conflict resolution.

In less formal conflicts, success in the competitive resolution process depends upon one's ability to trade concessions that satisfy the needs of both parties. For example, imagine that you and your significant other are in conflict about where to go on your two weeks of vacation this year. You prefer visiting locations that have historic value and like to tour old homes, museums, and antique stores, and you detest beach vacations baking in the sun. Your significant other, who is intolerant of "learning" vacations, prefers resorts and relaxing by the pool or on the beach, with a game of tennis or golf thrown in for good measure.

During the resolution process, each of you would stake your claim and insist that the other party consider your idea of vacation because it has more value. Each would use persuasive skills to try to convince the other to devote two weeks to the preferred type of vacation. Winning ultimately depends upon who is most persuasive and what you were willing to trade to get your preferred vacation. The resolution also may result in a compromise solution, or a splitting of the difference, where you might spend one week in the Virgin Islands and the other week in Boston. In other words, neither of you would "win" because each would be dissatisfied for one week of the two. Finally, some of the more creative thinkers might recognize a third, alternative solution—to go to Mexico or the Italian Riviera, where one could bask in the sun while the other toured ruins and museums. This type of innovation, however, would require willingness on the part of the competing parties to break out of their positional mode.

The competitive bargaining process is unappealing to many of us and often produces unwise agreements. Some of us simply do not have the skills or the temperament to play the game. We see the process as being unnecessarily tough, deceitful, or manipulative. Perceptions of power and control also are a significant factor in the effectiveness of competitive bargaining. If you do not have power in the relationship, or if you perceive that you do not, you are more likely to obtain an unsatisfactory resolution. Your lack of power will prevent you from using authority or aggression to resolve, or win, the dispute. In competitive bargaining, this form of aggression is often played as a trump card to achieve the win for the party who is able to acquire the most power.

The positional approach of competitive bargaining also causes unnecessary issue rigidity. Our egos become so invested in our positions that we are prevented from accepting alternatives. Therefore, even if a better solution is created, it is unlikely that we will back down. Once our egos are invested, we have to prove ourselves right to the other party because we fear losing that party's respect if we change our position. Consequently, we expend additional effort that further locks us into our unwise position in order to save face. The real danger is that as we put additional effort into defending our position, we put less effort into identifying whether our interests, let alone the other party's interests, are being satisfied. The result is often an agreement that has solved the wrong problem and is not satisfactory over the long term.

Another problem with competitive bargaining is that it often ignores the personal issues that affect the resolution process. In competitive bargaining, we care about the other party's needs only as a means to identify an opportunity for trade. For example, we will trade one day at the beach (the other party's need) for one day visiting museums (our need). But even if the trade satisfies one need, competitive bargaining still requires some amount of persuasion, deception, and manipulation if we are going to resolve all of the objective issues in a satisfactory manner. Over time, this usually breaks down the trust between the parties and places a significant strain on the relationship. If the relationship was shaky to begin with, the competitive process may prevent either party from engaging in the interaction at all.

In one such quarrel, two brothers were trying to settle their mother's estate after her death. Her will was sufficiently vague that the brothers had to work out the distribution of her tangible assets between themselves. The brothers had a history of conflict, and had not said more than a few words to each other over the course of many years. Not surprisingly, this situation only added to the tension.

They approached the resolution using competitive bargaining, and each staked his claim to various items in their mother's house. Of course, there were many items that appeared on both lists, so they pleaded their case, argued, and bickered. They feigned interest in some items in order to trade them for the things they really wanted. But in the end, they were no closer to agreement, and, to top it off, the intensity of the dispute started to affect their families. Eventually, their wives got together and brought in an outside party to end the process. The items were distributed, but neither conflict was truly resolved.

Competitive bargaining tends not to resolve conflict. It merely manages it for the short term. It is based on an attitude of limits and is fundamentally a process of reaching a settlement within a bargaining range. Both parties know that they are going to have to settle for something less than they would prefer, but they each hope that the deal will be better than their bottom line. Parties who do not think they got the best deal possible or who believe that they "lost" typically try to find ways to recoup their losses later. Even if one party believes that it "won," it still knows that it left something on the bargaining table and will try to acquire it in future negotiations. Labor and management, for example, may reach an agreement, but it is not long before they are back at the bargaining table, renegotiating issues that one or both sides thought had been settled previously.

The competitive bargaining process invites future conflict because it creates *compromise*. In the dual-concerns model, compromise is the middle ground where neither side wins or loses on the objective issues of the dispute. But compromise usually does not manage or resolve the personal issues. It very often creates additional personal issues because of the deception, power plays, and gamesmanship that accompany the process. Therefore, the parties frequently walk away from the table *feeling* that they have lost even if they achieved a better outcome than they expected. At the very least, they walk away harboring uncertainty about their association with the other party. This tends to weaken interaction over the longer term by establishing a relationship based on mutual suffering or "getting even" in the future.

There is an alternative that breaks the destructive cycle of competitive bargaining. It builds relationships and opens the door to constructive resolution. The alternative not only helps you correctly identify the objective issues, but also manages, if not resolves, the personal issues in the dispute. It is based on principles of interaction that endeavor to understand all of the underlying interests that must be satisfied to reach sustained agreement.

Collaboration

The *collaborative* approach to conflict resolution, also called *mutual gains* or *integrative bargaining*, argues for the possibility of solutions that all sides find acceptable. It embodies the notion of "win-win," a core component of our principle of mutual gain. Collaboration is about identifying a common, shared, or joint goal and developing a process to achieve it. It is a process in which both parties exchange information openly, define their common problems, and create options to solve these problems. And while the collaborative process cannot guarantee that agreement will always be reached, more often than not, the analysis of interests, needs, and desires helps the resolution process and ultimate agreement.

There are many reasons why people don't pursue this model of conflict resolution. First, *people in conflict often do not recognize the potential for collaboration.* This often is the result of an attitude of limits, either-or thinking, or a fixed-pie mentality. When parties remain positional or see only a limited number of solutions that will satisfy their interests, they do not use their creativity to solve the problem. The parties also suffer from issue rigidity and are unable to see beyond the investment they have made in their position. Their position and their perception of the other party's position appear incongruent, and they refuse to listen for underlying interests and needs. Collaboration is difficult when the parties believe that competition is the only way to resolve the issue; they usually cannot see that change results in new opportunity.

The *history of the relationship* between the two parties also can prevent collaboration. Over time, destructive conflict can build resentment, if not contempt. And, as John Gottman notes in *Why Marriages Succeed or Fail* (1994), contempt breeds the intent to "insult and psychologically abuse" the other party. This is not always major abuse; it may be small, nit-picking criticisms that add up over time. The personal issues become so overwhelming that the objective issues of the conflict cannot be examined, and parties often cannot be in the same room together, let alone identify ways of resolving the conflict.

Another barrier to collaboration relates to the *complexity of most conflicts.* Some elements are conducive to collaboration, and some elements require competitive bargaining. Each mode of conflict resolution requires different skill sets, and you can send mixed messages unless you handle them carefully. Suppose, for example, you wanted a raise from $25,000 to $30,000 because you had made significant contributions to your organization's objectives over the previous eighteen months. You also knew of organizations that were offering salaries ranging from $28,000 to $32,000 for the same work. The organization and you share the common goals of working to improve the success and profitability of the company and recognizing you for outstanding accomplishment. However, the specific amount of the salary increase may be an area of competition because the company has budget constraints and restrictive policies regarding salary increases. Both parties in this example probably recognize that the collaborative issues are more important because recognition of employees contributes to their commitment to a high level of performance. However, the differences in the competitive positions between your request for $30,000 and what the organization was willing or able to pay, $28,000, may create a barrier to a collaborative solution.

Finally, people often have a *lack of faith in their problem-solving ability*. Parties who enter the resolution process believing that they can work together usually find a way to collaborate. Those who do not have a solid self-concept will be less willing to follow the principles of interaction and use listening to seek collaborative resolution. People who do not have faith in their ability to collaborate are likely to slip back to their noncollaborative habits and compete, accommodate, or withdraw.

There are many obstacles that make collaboration more difficult. Given our inherent competitiveness and the various factors that surround many of our disputes, it is a wonder that constructive collaboration occurs at all. However, it does occur if one or both of the parties in conflict maintain self-awareness, follow the principles of interaction, and stick with the listening-based, collaborative process. In order to achieve constructive outcomes, the following conditions must be established at some point during the process:

- *Face-to-face interaction.* The Listening to Conflict approach to dispute resolution requires developing an understanding of the total message another party is trying to communicate. The most effective way to accomplish this is through face-to-face interaction, where we can see the nonverbal expressions that give us clues to underlying emotional needs.
- *High acquaintance potential.* Without the ability to accept and have positive regard for the other party, collaboration will not be possible. We have to like the person as a person and be willing to establish a relationship that goes

beyond the issues of the dispute. This will allow the personal issues to be dealt with separately from the objective issues in the particular conflict so that we can explore options for mutual gain.

- *Constituency support.* The parties in conflict will not be able to collaborate if outside constituencies try to force competitive and positional norms. Third parties must be supportive of the collaborative process or risk nullifying the positive steps taken toward collaboration by reneging on constructive agreements established between the two interacting parties. We must prevent or resolve any conflict with our constituencies prior to interacting with the other party in the primary dispute.

- *Cooperative tasks.* Acceptance goes a long way toward diffusing head-to-head competition in conflict, but unless a joint or mutual task is established, there will be no need to collaborate. We at least must frame the conflict as a problem to be solved together in order to establish a collaborative environment.

- *Shared exploration.* Sharing in the process of understanding the problem and creating solutions keeps both parties involved. This saves one party from the trap of inventing all of the solutions, and the inevitable dependence and resentment that accompanies that responsibility. When both parties are involved, there will be stronger commitment to the final solutions.

- *No fixed agenda.* An agenda creates a positional interaction that is based on satisfying the needs of one party without understanding how the interests of both are related. Having an agenda sends the message that you are not interested in the other party's issues and needs. The only agenda should be to follow the steps of collaboration and work toward mutual gain.

- *Adherence to collaborative process steps.* Successful resolution requires that we follow the steps of collaboration. If we skip a step, we risk sending the other party mixed signals that will propel that party toward a defensive, competitive mode.

Of course, it goes without saying that in addition to the above elements, the parties also must maintain self-awareness and the principles of interaction. The combination ensures that we establish a different atmosphere for the relationship. It may take two parties to start a conflict, but it takes only one disciplined, patient, and principled individual to transform competition into collaboration.

The Six Steps of Collaboration

With the above conditions in mind, a constructive environment can be established. However, collaboration also requires that resolution proceed through a series of steps that create a more effective interaction. Each step is an important ingredient of the relationship-building process that leads to creative solutions built upon mutual gain. The steps progress logically and should be departed from only to return to a previous step as a means to enhance the relationship and increase understanding. Skipping steps reduces the chance for collaborative agreement and should be avoided. The six steps to collaborative conflict resolution follow (see Figure 5-1).

Figure 5-1. The six steps of collaboration.

1. Prepare for the Interaction
2. Initiate the Exchange.
3. Facilitate the Relationship.
4. Understand the Interests.
5. Examine the Solutions.
6. Reach Consensus.

Step 1. Prepare for the Interaction

Whatever type of conflict we hope to resolve, lack of preparation can hurt the interaction. Whether the conflict is an ongoing controversy or a new dispute, an office quarrel or a domestic argument, a few moments of focused attention prior to the interaction will improve our effectiveness. Even if we are highly skilled and experienced in the resolution process, preparation for the current situation will help us remain constructive throughout the interaction.

Preparation does take time, but it also helps prevent problems that could occur throughout the resolution process. It gives us the big-picture perspective that we need if we are to maintain self-awareness and composure. It helps us assess the interpersonal zones of both parties so that we can keep communication positive. It also will help us think through the issues of the conflict and try to come to an initial understanding of the interests involved for both parties. You should plan to spend almost as much time preparing for the interaction as you expect to spend resolving the conflict with the other party.

Recognize that in many respects, a listening mode is a form of preparation. When we listen, we gather information that might help shed new light on the conflict. When someone confronts us and forces us to deal with the conflict on the spot (which often escalates tensions), maintaining a detached, listening posture neutralizes the potential destructiveness of the interaction. Once the emotional intensity has decreased, we can request a time-out to consider the information just presented and to restore any emotional imbalance that was created by the sudden confrontation.

However, listening should not be substituted for true preparation. In other words, we should not listen, then immediately take the next step in the resolution process. We risk being caught off guard, not having thought through all of the interests that need to be satisfied—the other party's and ours—and the external factors that may influence the outcome. We also risk solving the wrong problem because we have not properly diagnosed.

There is no right way to prepare, but we should make sure that our thoughts are organized and that we are ready to maintain a constructive discourse. Until you develop your own preparation process, walk through the following checklist before you engage in conflict resolution. It should help you consider each aspect of your conflict.

Interpersonal Zones

- What are your comfort zones?
- What are your hot zones?
- What are your values?

- Are you extraverted or introverted?
- What are your needs for inclusion, control, and affection?
- How do you gather, sift, and act on information?
- How will you have to adapt or modify your behavior to be effective with the other party?

- What are the other party's comfort zones?
- What are the other party's hot zones?
- What are the other party's observable values?
- Is the other party extraverted or introverted?
- What are the other party's needs for inclusion, control, and affection?
- How does the other party gather, sift, and act on information?
- Is the other party typically competitive or collaborative?

Factors Affecting the Conflict

- What is the nature of the disagreement? Consider both objective and personal issues.
- What is the position of each party? What are the stated and unstated goals? What does each party hope to accomplish?
- What interests, needs, or motivations are represented by the positions? What does each party care about?
- If you were in the other party's shoes, what would you want?
- What do you and the other party have in common? Where are you already in agreement?

- What additional information, data, or expertise do you need in order to understand the issues in this conflict?
- What constituencies will influence the interaction? (Conduct a preparation analysis of each constituency identified.)
- What will happen if you can't resolve the conflict? How will each party satisfy its interests?
- Do you want to resolve the conflict? Or should you cut your ties and find an alternative solution?

Nature of the Relationship

- What is the history of the relationship?
- Will this be an ongoing relationship?
- Why might the present working relationship be difficult?
- Who has more power? Where do you each have power?
- Do you each have the authority to make and follow through on commitments?
- What else will you have to do to make your agreement work?
- What will you need to do to make sure the resolution process helps the relationship?

Step 2. Initiate the Exchange

As you have no doubt experienced, the other party will not always initiate the conflict-resolution process. Sometimes it is our problem and we need to confront the other party. Just because we have identified an issue that is of concern to us does not mean that the other party is consciously aware of a problem. Other times, people's orientation to conflict or the composition of their social zones may reduce their desire or ability to confront us. They may not understand the specific problem, or they may lack conflict-management skills. Whatever the reason, we often have to initiate an exchange that engages the other party in a discussion of the conflict. How we communicate our problem will determine whether the confrontation escalates the tensions or keeps the resolution constructive. Consider the following example.

> Dorothy, a manager in the purchasing department of a midsize manufacturing company, had a problem with the job performance of one of her employees, Noelle. In particular, Noelle had not completed a vendor analysis by the deadline they had established. This was yet another in a series of problems that Dorothy believed Noelle had with time management. She had not confronted Noelle directly about this before because she thought that if she emphasized the deadlines when she gave the assignments to Noelle, Noelle would "get it." However, after many missed deadlines, Dorothy felt that the time had come to confront Noelle about the problem. Although she was upset that Noelle had not completed the report on time, she was mostly irritated that Noelle had not talked to her in advance about the delays.
>
> "Noelle, you haven't given me the vendor analysis yet. I should have known, given the problems we've had before with deadlines, that it might be too much for you. When can I expect it?"
>
> "But Dorothy," Noelle responded, "I am still waiting for returns on the quality measures from some departments. I can't finish it until . . ."
>
> "Well, why didn't you tell me this before? I could have helped get that information to you or shown you how to get it yourself. You never talk to me about these things. You've got to let me know."

Let's assume that Noelle really does have significant problems with time management that cause her to miss deadlines, and that some of those misses have had tangible costs. Let's also assume that Dorothy has spoken to Noelle about this before and is at her wit's end. And finally, let's agree that at some level, Dorothy has every right to express her frustration to Noelle, if not fire her. However, if Dorothy's objective was to solve the problem, will her approach to initiating the exchange promote constructive interaction? Probably not.

The secret to constructive resolution is not solving the problems that caused the dispute, but rather managing the emotions that are stirred up by the conflict. The confrontation process, therefore, must incorporate the principles of interaction in order to break the cycle of negativity that intensifies the conflict. We must engage in face-to-face interaction that communicates mutual respect, shared exploration, and commitment to resolution without a fixed agenda.

One of the more significant reasons conflicts turn into destructive battles is that we avoid them. We are afraid of hurting others' feelings, injuring others' self-confidence, or being impolite, and sometimes we are not sure whether it is a problem of theirs or a problem of ours. So, rather than confront the other person about the issue, we sit on it. We wait and ponder it. But by the time the objective issue comes up again, we have let it fester in our subconscious until it becomes intermingled with a new personal issue. Now not only are we upset about whatever the problem may be, we also are angry with the other person.

For example, when Dorothy finally confronted Noelle, she included statements such as, "I should have known . . . that it might be too much for you" and "You never . . ." While this may have expressed Dorothy's emotions about Noelle, it contributed to a destructive resolution. Dorothy did not maintain detached responsibility. She did not initiate the exchange in a way that expressed acceptance or a desire for mutual gain.

The process of initiating the exchange contains three steps:

1. Confront.
2. Involve.
3. Problem-solve.

Confront.   *Confronting* requires that you let the other party know that you have an issue you want to discuss, but also requires that you communicate this in a supportive, open-ended manner. When we confront, we must communicate the problem, but also demonstrate our continued desire to listen to the other party. We also should tell the other party *our* problem, not the problem we are having with *him or her*. In other words, we should state the result, or our emotion or feeling, and the situation that caused the result, the issue, or behavior. Use the "I" message instead of the "you" message. For example,

> *Say:* "I am upset that I did not receive the vendor analysis, Noelle."
> *Instead of:* "You did not give me the vendor analysis yet."

"I am upset" is the result, our feeling about the situation. "I did not receive the vendor analysis" is the situation that caused the result. "You did not give me the vendor analysis yet" may be accurate, but risks putting Noelle on the defensive. Once the other party goes on the defensive, *we* have transformed an objective issue into a personal issue. Here is another example:

> *Say:* "I wish you would keep me informed."
> *Instead of:* "Why didn't you tell me that?"

"I wish" is the result, our feeling about the situation, and "you would keep me informed" is the behavior we want from the other party to prevent the problem. The second statement backs the other party into a corner and competitively dares her or him to provide an acceptable answer. Instead of "You are the problem," the "I" confrontation communicates "I have a problem and I need your help." It asks the other party to collaborate—to be involved in the resolution.

Involve. The reason we Listen to Conflict is to *involve* the other party, the next part of the confrontation process. By involving the other party, we ask for that party's perspective, opinion, feedback, and help. The involve statements need to be open-ended and nonjudgmental. For example,

> *Confront:* "I am upset that I did not receive the vendor analysis, Noelle."
> *Involve:* "Help me understand what's going on."
> *or*
> *Involve:* "Tell me what problems you are encountering."

Instead of: "Why haven't I received it?" (competitive dare)

or

Instead of: "Do you need any help?" ("You are incapable")

We involve the other party for three important reasons. First, we may not have all the information we need in order to understand the problem. We cannot determine the options for resolution until we hear all sides of the story. Second, if we want the other party's commitment to the resolution, that party must participate in the process of creating that resolution. When someone is involved, it becomes that person's idea, and he or she is more likely to follow through on the action plan that is developed. And finally, when we involve, we communicate our acceptance of the other party. We are letting that party know that she or he is important and capable, and that we want her or his help in identifying and solving the problem.

Problem-Solve.   The final element required to initiate the exchange is to *problem-solve*. Once we have the other party's involvement, we listen for that party's perspectives, needs, and interests, and we invite his or her analysis of the situation. We ask the question, "What are your thoughts and ideas?" Then, we identify the objective, create and explore the options for resolution, establish criteria for a solution, and decide.

The confront–involve–problem-solve model used to initiate the exchange is, in a sense, a simplified version of the six steps of collaboration. Step 1, Prepare for the Interaction, and step 2, Initiate the Exchange, are the equivalent of confronting. These steps establish a mind-set and environment for collaboration prior to the stages that are more directly related to resolving the conflict. The next two steps, facilitate the relationship and understand the interests, relate directly to the application of listening in order to involve the other party, while examine the options and reach consensus embody problem solving. This comparison is drawn to show the similarity of the two models and to demonstrate how the concepts surrounding listening-based collaboration can be applied throughout the conflict-resolution process.

Step 3. Facilitate the Relationship

In order for collaboration to succeed, both parties must be motivated to work together rather than compete. One can initiate the process, but eventually both must be in the collaborative mode in order to achieve resolution. They both must focus on understanding the individual interests and needs that must be satisfied to reach resolution. They also must attend to both the objective issues and the personal issues as they try to identify mutual goals and objectives. However, for collaboration to truly be effective, they both must adopt a personal style that is conducive to collaboration.

The collaborative relationship is characterized primarily by open communication and trust. When both parties in conflict communicate openly and honestly, their needs and concerns can be identified. This provides the information required to shift the conflict from a positional dispute to interest-based problem solving. Interestingly, open communication by one party creates open communication by the other. This often is referred to as *reciprocating self-disclosure,* meaning that the more you reveal about yourself, in terms of both the degree and the depth of disclosure, the more the other party will reveal to you.

A study conducted by Zick Rubin (1975) demonstrates this idea. Students approached individual passengers waiting in a lounge of Boston's Logan Airport and asked them for assistance in a study of handwriting. A student would write a few sentences that described himself or herself, then ask the passengers to write a few sentences describing themselves. In some cases, the student wrote a sentence of low intimacy, such as, "I am in the process of collecting handwriting samples," while in other cases, the student wrote a sentence of high intimacy, such as, "I think I am well adjusted, but I occasionally have some questions about my adequacy."

Passengers were found to reciprocate based on the level of intimacy in the statement. If a student wrote a statement of high intimacy, the passenger's statement was generally longer and more intimate. However, Rubin also found that the tendency to reciprocate applied only when the students appeared to be composing the sentence *spontaneously*. There was no reciprocation if the students appeared to be writing a standard statement written by someone else. Thus, open communication must be a natural part of our principles of interaction and not a technique used to manipulate the other party.

Other researchers have found similar results, suggesting that when one person takes a leading role in self-disclosure, others will follow this lead (Davis, 1976; Lynn, 1977). One explanation is that our disclosure sends the message that we like and trust the others. Consequently, they feel better about themselves, and in turn feel more confident revealing their interests and needs (Taylor, Gould, and Brounstein, 1981). In contrast, when people do not trust one another, they are more likely to engage in competitive bargaining, use threats, and become positional (Kimel, Pruitt, Magenau, Konar-Goldband, and Carnevale, 1980). They also are likely to become more defensive and competitive, attacking the issues raised by others (Gibb, 1961). While the existence of trust in a relationship does not always guarantee collaboration, the absence of trust increases the chance of competition. For trust to develop effectively, the relationship must be nurtured.

Collaborative relationships also appear to be enhanced when each party believes he or she is benefiting from the interaction. Social exchange theorists suggest that most social relationships can be viewed in terms of costs and benefits. They suggest that in order to maintain a given relationship, we carefully evaluate the things we must do for the other person compared to the satisfaction that we receive. We weigh these costs and benefits against our subjective picture of a satisfactory relationship, a picture developed out of past experiences with others and our knowledge of what other relationships are like. We primarily use our current reference groups as the basis for this comparison, comparing others to our friends, family, professional relationships, and established relationships within our social-cultural groups.

Another factor that significantly strengthens the collaborative relationship is familiarity. A number of researchers have demonstrated that we tend to like those with whom we are familiar. The more we are exposed to someone, the greater the probability that we will like that person. This is especially true if we experienced positive emotions around that other person, whether she or he caused the emotions or not (Clore and Byrne, 1974). These exposure effects occur even when people are shown stimuli that they do not recognize consciously as something they have seen before (Moreland and Zajonc, 1979). It appears we often grow to like people who just happen to be close at hand (Ebbesen, Kjob, and Konecni, 1976; Festinger, Schachter, and Back, 1950).

Bob, a senior vice president in charge of information systems for a major U.S. bank, once described an action plan he created for two employees who were not getting along. The two vice presidents were not on speaking terms, and their troubled relationship had infiltrated and soured the entire IS organization. Bob had had many one-on-one sessions with each of them in which he tried to provide conflict-resolution coaching, but the relationship between the two senior-level managers did not improve.

Finally, he called them both into his office and said, "I am frustrated because I have not been effective in helping either of you. We've talked about a number of approaches that, from your reports, don't seem to be working. I value both of your individual contributions, and I want to make this work. Here is what I want you to do: For the next two months, I want you to schedule a lunch together once per week. The company will pay for it, but I have ground rules: You are not allowed to talk about business. Talk about your personal lives, your hobbies, your families, your interests, but no business. In two months, we'll meet again to see how things are going."

At the first lunch, they were both resistant, and not much was discussed for the first half-hour of the meal. They picked at their food and said very few words. However, during the second half-hour they decided to try it and began to talk about everything from their kids' activities to their golf games. They started to open up on a personal level and realized that they had much in common. After their third lunch, they returned to Bob's office elated because, although they had broken his "no business conversation" rule, they had talked constructively for the first time about the objective issues causing the dispute.

In order to facilitate the relationship during conflict, we must demonstrate a willingness to be open, and demonstrate that we trust the other party by sharing meaningful information about ourselves that may leave us vulnerable. We also need to create a positive and supportive emotional environment so that others feel good for having interacted with us. We can accomplish this by listening and trying to understand their issues, interests, and needs. And finally, we must interact frequently. The interests and needs that we share personally build a common sense of purpose that make the objective issues much easier to manage.

Step 4. Understand the Interests

The fourth step of the collaborative process, understand the interests, accomplishes two important tasks that are critical to ultimate resolution. First, we *learn the underlying interests and needs* that are important to the other party and that must be satisfied if constructive resolution is to occur. We identify *why* the other party wants what he or she wants. Second, we *establish the criteria for solutions*. In other words, we identify *how we will know* if the agreement has satisfied the important interests.

Of the steps in the collaborative resolution process, it is in the fourth step that our listening skills are most important. Understanding is the process of becoming aware of all the cues that the other party emits. It requires openness to the other party's communication. It also requires that we go beyond the stated positions and demands to learn what needs, values, and interests motivate the demands. We must listen to both the apparent and the unapparent, the conscious and the subconscious, because often a message carries both a visible and a hidden meaning that contradict each other. For example, I might say what I think I should say or what I think you want to hear—"I am not angry." However, my red face, clenched fists, and locked jaw reveal otherwise. This may be a deliberate attempt to mask my emotions, or I may not be aware of how I really feel. For constructive conflict resolution to occur, we must listen to all cues and encourage others to open communication channels that ordinarily are not used.

Remember that the definition of conflict implies that the problem in conflict resolution is the result of *perceived* incompatibility. By going beyond positional demands, we uncover the needs and interests that we may hold in common with the other party. We often assume that if the other party's demands are opposed to ours, he or she must have an entirely different need structure or set of objectives. Conflicts over goals are always more challenging to resolve than conflicts over means. For example, consider a conflict involving a husband and wife disagreeing about household financial issues. If they both want to minimize debt in an effort to work toward early retirement, they are far more likely to resolve differences surrounding purchases or investment decisions. On the other hand, if one is inclined toward savings and the other prefers a life of more immediate gratification, conflicts about money will pose more significant obstacles to overcome. However, unless they make an effort to understand each other's underlying interests and needs, the two types of conflicts may look and feel the same.

Another illustration of how this may work can be provided by a simplified example of two countries in a border dispute. The borders had been redrawn fifty years earlier after a war in which Country B had acquired land that had previously belonged to Country A. Country A has a competitive orientation and makes a positional demand:

> *Country A:* "We want the border that separates your country from our country redrawn. We insist that you return land that is rightfully ours."

Based on a competitive, or positional, approach to conflict, if Country B gives up the land and redraws the border, Country A will perceive that it "won." If B does not give up the land and redraw the border, A will perceive that it "lost" (although, in reality, the conflict would not stop after that brief exchange). For the time being, we will not worry about how B defines its win.

Obviously, if B replies by saying, "No, we will not return the land," then the two countries are fully engaged in a competitive interaction. Since B wants to arrive at a solution based on mutual gain, it needs to try to go beyond the position in order to understand the interests behind that position. B responds empathically by saying,

> *Country B:* "It sounds as if you feel that the border is unfair and you have lost part of your history. You would like the land that was formerly yours returned to your nation."

In reality, disputes between countries, ethnic groups, or religious factions are never resolved easily. However, continued attempts to posture and persuade only add to the intensity of conflicts that have already been fueled by cultural differences and issue rigidity. By taking a listening-based approach to understanding the interests, B increases the chances of working A toward collaboration. If B comes right out and denies the request or asks, "Why?!" it is likely that A will become defensive. Asking the direct question too early in the process risks establishing an environment that forces the other party to dig in its heels and become even more positional and competitive. Reflecting, repeating, and rephrasing is more likely to lead the other party to reveal the successive layers of interests and needs that must be satisfied in seeking a solution that achieves mutual gain.

The empathic response is important because it demonstrates acceptance and confirms understanding. The competitive walls begin to break down once the other party perceives that we understand its perspective. The other party begins to think of us as a partner that provides assistance, rather than as an adversary that prevents attainment of its goals. Another important reason for responding in this fashion is that it subtly prompts the other party to tell us more and explain. For example, Country B might learn that Country A did not really want the border redrawn, it wanted restitution for war damages. Country B might also learn that Country A actually wanted access to the natural resources located in that parcel of land to boost its ailing economy. The process would reveal that Country A has interests that go beyond the positional demand regarding borderlines.

Accordingly, step 4, understanding the interests, helps us properly diagnose the real problem, rather than settle on a compromise among the divergent positions. It ensures that before we solve the problem, we bring all interests to the surface so that we can establish the criteria for the eventual solutions.

The second aspect of understanding the interests is to identify the yardsticks by which our ultimate agreement will be measured. As W. Edwards Deming suggested, "If you can't measure it, you can't improve it." In other words, if we hope to reach long-lasting, constructive resolution, we need a tool to make sure that the agreed-upon solutions do, in fact, satisfy the identified interests. We need standards and objective measures that will allow both parties to know that they are meeting their part of the agreement.

The criteria for solutions should be established *before* we begin to solve the problem. The standards will provide an objective basis that will help us determine whether we have an effective solution. By establishing criteria, we also help prevent personal issues from negatively affecting our resolution. For example, there have no doubt been times when you did not have a "good gut feel" about a solution. The objective information appeared to lead to a given conclusion, but your intuition told you otherwise. Since explaining gut feel can be difficult, other parties tend to think we are concealing information or acting stubborn. If we have previously established the expected results and performance criteria, we are better able to explain the logic behind the intuition. Or, if we still cannot explain our logic, having established criteria gives the other parties the tools to understand how our intuition may produce the desired results. Objective criteria also help us establish fair standards and procedures for conducting our resolution process.

Suppose a husband and wife are arguing over household financial issues. The husband is angry with his wife because they do not have enough money for him to "play the market," and he claims it is because she is a spendthrift. The wife is angry with her husband because he put her in charge of paying the bills and she does not feel that he gives her credit for managing their finances and balancing the checkbook. His demand is that she give him the checkbook responsibilities and all her credit cards. Her demand is that he stop harassing her.

Neither initiated the exchange in a constructive manner, but after some time facilitating the relationship, they were ready to try to understand the interests. After listening empathically, the wife learned that her husband really did not want to pay the bills and manage the checkbook. However, she also learned that he was afraid that if they did not get their financial issues straightened out, he would not be able to live his dream of retiring early and sailing the Caribbean. He also was concerned about their relationship. He told her that at times he felt abandoned by her because she did not seem to share his dream.

The husband learned that his wife was afraid that their debt and expenses would overtake them, and she did not want to feel the embarrassment and shame of declaring bankruptcy. He also learned that she felt unappreciated for her efforts to manage their money.

Initially, they saw the conflict as a positional argument over who would gain control of the checkbook and credit cards. Had the conflict been resolved competitively, there would have been a clear winner and loser. However, after listening to each other and trying to understand the interests, they realized that they shared a number of common concerns (Figure 5-2). Both shared the common objective interests of reducing their debt and expenses while increasing their savings. The husband had the additional interests of working toward living his dream (and reducing the feeling of fear associated with not achieving that objective) and reestablishing the connection with his wife (and reducing the feeling of abandonment associated with perceiving that his wife did not share his goals). The wife had the additional interests of wanting to feel appreciated for her efforts and reducing the fear of financial failure.

Figure 5-2. Personal and objective interests in a
dispute over family financial issues.

	Interests	Criteria
Husband	*Personal* 1. Live his dream (*fear*) 2. Reestablish connection (*abandonment*) *Objective* 1. Reduce debt and expenses 2. Increase savings	*Personal* 1. Increase in days spent sailing 2. Resolved through interaction *Objective* 1. Total dollar amount of debt and expenses 2. Total dollar amount of savings
Wife	*Personal* 1. Feel *appreciated* 2. Reduce *fear* of bankruptcy *Objective* 1. Reduce debt and expenses 2. Increase savings	*Personal* 1. Resolved through interaction 2. Total dollar amount of debt and expenses *Objective* 1. Total dollar amount of debt and expenses 2. Total dollar amount of savings

At this stage, most people jump right to the obvious solution of a budget and a savings plan to resolve the objective issues. Consequently, they do not establish criteria that will tell them whether that is the right solution. They also neglect to manage the important personal issues that are identified, and they risk having to revisit these issues as part of a different conflict. For example, in a separate conflict over housework, the husband still may feel abandoned and the wife unappreciated unless they have established criteria that provide feedback about their improvement. When personal issues are not addressed, they tend to grow in intensity and become attached to other issues down the road.

In this example, the husband and wife decided that the criteria to measure debt and expense reduction would be to assess the reduction in the total dollar amount of their debt and expenses and in various subcategories, such as mortgage, automobile, student loans, and credit cards. They decided that the criteria for increased savings also would be to assess a total dollar figure. In addition, the couple decided that the solution to these objective issues, at least on the initial pass, should include not having to sell their house to achieve the objectives.

Identifying criteria for the personal interests is much more challenging, but not always necessary. Very often, the process of Listening to Conflict provides the emotional release needed to resolve the personal issues surrounding a specific set of objective issues. In this specific conflict, for example, the husband determined that they did not have to identify criteria for "reestablishing the connection" because he felt that the conversations to resolve the objective issues had helped him to feel, at least for now, back on track with his wife. Likewise, the wife indicated that the conflict-resolution process had helped her realize that her husband did appreciate her efforts and that he shared her fears. Accordingly, she did not think that her personal issues needed further solving at this time. As for the husband's need to live his dream, they both decided that they could assess progress on that interest by gauging debt and expense reduction, savings increases, and the number of additional days per year he (they) spent sailing.

Identifying objective criteria is the last step in understanding the interests because it confirms to both parties that they have mutual understanding. When an objective measurement system can be established, both parties are counting the same things. This creates a collaborative process for ensuring that the solutions created and defined in steps 5 and 6 work toward satisfying those interests. When the other person feels that we understand him or her both conceptually and emotionally, we create an important emotional bond. This trust increases cooperation and allows each party to reveal important information that helps us establish the criteria for constructive resolution.

Step 5. Examine the Solutions

The essence of constructive conflict is valuing and utilizing differences. This does not imply that we have to agree with the other party's perspective, only that we must respect it and see it as important for long-term results. These differences help us create interdependent solutions that are better than those we could produce alone. When both parties feel understood and respected, collaborative solutions begin to flow.

"Solutions" is plural for a variety of reasons. First, our principles of interaction are founded upon an attitude of abundance that suggests that there are innumerable solutions to all problems. While some options are often easier to see or more preferable than others, until we create choices, we are playing a win-lose game. If there is only one solution, we risk having one or both parties walk away from the agreement feeling less than satisfied. We probably have overlooked important personal and objective interests. Next, a good outcome must satisfy the different interests of both parties. If we want to make sure that we have found the optimal agreement, we need to explore the many possible agreements and pieces of agreement.

The search for solutions is the creative phase of the collaborative process. Once we understand the interests and have established the criteria for solution, we must generate a variety of possible options that solve the identified problems. We want to formulate as many ideas as possible so that we can examine our options from a variety of angles and consider the various combinations that may result.

There are a number of techniques that can help us maximize our creative potential and generate a wealth of solutions. We might choose to *brainstorm* and invent as many possible solutions as we can in a spontaneous, free flowing manner. Brainstorming focuses on the possibilities, no matter how impractical they may seem, and we are encouraged not to judge them as unworkable, unrealistic, too expensive, or too abstract. In addition, we should not discuss, expand on, or criticize ideas when they are presented, so that the momentum of creativity can continue. The brainstorming process should be exhaustive and should not stop after the current conflict-resolution session or even after we have "resolved" the problem. Creativity tends to generate more creativity. Often the best or breakthrough ideas are created as we gain more experience satisfying particular issues in the conflict.

Another terrific strategy for identifying solutions is to invite third parties into the process (discussed in Chapter 6). These individuals or groups can provide needed expertise or provide a fresh look at the problem. Sometimes we need others who have nothing invested in the outcome to help us get beyond mental blocks to certain solutions. Their perspective may provide the insight we need to generate additional options for resolution.

Once we have identified a variety of solutions, we need to expand, combine, separate, evaluate, analyze, rip apart, and otherwise put them to the test. We need to examine all of the solutions to ensure that we have not overlooked creative ways of satisfying our interests. When we perform a thorough analysis, we create a results-oriented process built upon a mutually agreed-upon end that allows us to reach consensus decisions.

Step 6. Reach Consensus

The principle of mutual gain requires that we do not finalize any agreement until we know that we have satisfied both parties. Therefore, the agreement must meet the legitimate needs of everyone and be perceived as fair. It should not be implemented fully if participants perceive that they compromised on an important issue or that their interests were not met. Consensus is achieved when each party in conflict:

- Feels that he or she has been heard and understood by the other.
- Is able to live with the decision or solution.
- Is willing to commit to his or her role during implementation.

Before we finalize the agreement, we should review the interests presented, the objectives identified, the criteria established, and the solution agreed upon. We should stop at each point and confirm that we have mutual understanding. This establishes that we are "on the same page," and will help prevent "buyer's remorse" and make each participant feel more secure about the results.

We should use our listening skills during this phase of conflict resolution to help manage the end of the agreement. At this stage, people want to end the process and go do other things. They see the light at the end of the tunnel and may want to rush out of the darkness. If this is the case, we want to make sure that they slow down a little bit. They are likely to agree to something that does not satisfy their needs simply to eliminate the stress of the interaction. We also have to guard against parties balking as we get to the end of our resolution process. If the conflict has been protracted and intense, agreement and resolution creates a new emotion for the parties to manage. Since they may be uncomfortable with this feeling of resolution, they often resist. In both cases we have to help manage emotions by continuing to demonstrate acceptance and using empathic listening to help them resolve their feelings.

At the same time, we must have heightened self-awareness. It is likely that we will feel some of the same emotions. We need to be sure we manage our own feelings as effectively as we help others manage theirs, so that we can make sure that the decision satisfies all of our interests.

The final step of reaching consensus is to gain commitment and establish an operating agreement. This does not necessarily mean that we put our agreement down in writing and legalese, but rather that we agree to the method for implementation and evaluation. This will help keep each of us committed to living up to our end of the agreement. It also keeps us committed to continuing to listen and to examine further and possibly better solutions as more information is presented over time.

During implementation, we should remain detached responsibly and not try to manage the other person's area of accountability. Let the other person choose whether or not to live up to her or his end of the agreement. If the other person chooses not to do so, we probably did not identify and work through a personal issue or interest that was important to that person. When we get back together to review, we should discuss it supportively and seek a new collaborative agreement that satisfies all of our concerns.

Remember that it is not the final decision, it is just the next decision.

Choosing an Approach

Collaboration may not be the best mode of conflict resolution in all situations. Take, for example, the process of determining a fair purchase price for a used car. Situations like buying a used car focus on a single issue, to be addressed only once, where you do not expect to see the other party ever again. The interests are simple: You want to pay as little as possible for as much car as possible, and the seller wants to maximize the return. There is no incentive to improve the relationship because you will never see the seller again after the transaction. Therefore, it is pointless to use empathic listening and engage in collaboration to resolve the final deal. It is probably more efficient to engage in competitive bargaining, right?

Suppose you had thoroughly researched the car you wanted to purchase and knew that its approximate market value was $10,000. When you arrived at the seller's home, the car was sitting out front looking polished and shiny, almost as if it had just come off the showroom floor. Still, you wanted to get a good deal, so you kicked the tires, checked under the hood, examined the interior, and took it for a test drive. Since you had told your friends that you were going to "negotiate like a pro," you also shook your head, looked concerned, and occasionally said, "Hmmm." When you finished your investigation, you turned to the seller and said, "I'll give you $8,000."

Now, you knew that this was not a fair price for the car, but you figured that when you made such a low offer, the seller would act surprised, maybe even chuckle, and come back with a counteroffer. Then the two of you would bargain back and forth until you arrived at a final deal that was better for you than the $10,000 market value. Well, the seller pursed his lips, sighed as if seriously pondering the offer, and said, "OK. Deal!"

Many thoughts might be running through your mind at this

stage. Your first thought would probably be, "Oh, no. What's wrong with this car?" After all, why would the seller be so quick to accept such an obviously low price? But after you have had a mechanic inspect the vehicle and you grow confident that it is not going to fall apart, you will probably start to think, "I should have tried to get a better deal!" It is also possible that you might start to feel guilty, wondering if somehow you had been unfair.

Even if in reality you achieved a great deal, you do not know if you should feel satisfied with the resolution. Although the mechanic said the car was in great shape, you will probably drive it cautiously for the first few months, waiting for something to go wrong. You do not know whether the seller knew about a problem that neither your mechanic nor you could identify. Or maybe the seller was fabulously wealthy and the proceeds from the sale did not matter to him—he just wanted to sell the car. It is also possible that the seller really was inexperienced and that your tough approach was unfair. Therefore, while you managed the objective issues of this conflict and negotiated a good deal, you failed to attend to the important personal issues that ultimately make you *feel* that it was a good deal.

The point of this example is not to suggest that the noncollaborative modes of conflict resolution should not be used under any circumstance, but rather to demonstrate how elements of collaboration, especially level 5 and level 6 listening, can be used to enhance all modes of conflict resolution. If you first engage in the six steps of the collaborative process, you will obtain the information that you need in order to determine whether a different mode of resolution would be more appropriate.

In reality, the six steps of conflict resolution are not a lock-step process. We may encounter resistance at any stage along the way and have to return to an earlier stage to facilitate the relationship or understand the interests. When you listen empathically to understand the other party's interests and needs before solving the problem of the conflict, you not only will be sure of solving the right problem, but also will maintain a constructive resolution environment that will produce a final agreement satisfying to both parties.

6
Collaboration Applied

The hour's now come;
The very minute bids thee ope thine ear.
Obey, and be attentive.

William Shakespeare, *The Tempest*

Sometimes, no matter how diligently we apply the Listening to Conflict principles and skills, we cannot seem to resolve our conflicts. We maintain self-awareness and understand our interpersonal zones. We exercise discipline, desire, and patience, and we are detached responsibly. We listen empathically and demonstrate acceptance and a desire for mutual gain. And we try to proceed through the six steps of collaboration. However, the other party to the conflict does not seem interested in a constructive resolution nor willing to collaborate toward consensus solutions.

There are many reasons why others do not collaborate. Some people may react so negatively to the history of their relationship with us or the history of the relationships they have with others that they are afraid and distrustful. They may have a poor self-concept and consequently lack self-awareness and self-mastery, or they may lack other cognitive abilities and skills required for constructive resolution. Some may perceive that they hold all the cards and do not see how collaborating would benefit them. And a few may be so highly competitive and driven by the rush of self-esteem they receive from winning that collaboration is not within the realm of possibility.

Disciplined application of the Listening to Conflict principles and skills will enhance all long-term interactions and help us understand, prevent, manage, and resolve the majority of the conflicts in our life. However, when we are not achieving constructive results, we sometimes need alternatives. Now and then, we need other choices that will help us satisfy our needs and move forward with a solution, but at the same time will not send inconsistent, unprincipled signals to the other party.

This chapter will provide some suggestions, techniques, and approaches to help you get beyond some of the problems you may encounter while trying to collaborate. In particular, it will describe two important collaborative tools to help break resistance to constructive resolution. This chapter also will answer some commonly asked questions regarding the Listening to Conflict method.

Find an Alternative Solution

The principle of mutual gain suggests that a constructive resolution should leave us better off than we were before. The objective issues and personal issues should be resolved in ways that satisfy the interests of both parties. Nevertheless, we know realistically that we may not always be able to reach a mutually satisfactory resolution with some parties. Our detached responsibility helps us understand that some things are beyond our control. Sometimes the complex, multi-issue nature of a conflict may prevent us from collaborating with the other party, either in whole or in part. We may agree on some issues and disagree on others. We may have the wherewithal to satisfy some interests, while others are beyond either party's capabilities.

Prior to entering the process of conflict resolution, we should know how we can satisfy our needs if we are not able to reach agreement with the other party. Otherwise, we risk being attached to the notion that we *must* resolve the conflict, even if the solution is destructive and unsatisfying. We should understand our alternative to collaboration so that we can protect ourselves from accepting an agreement that we should reject or rejecting an agreement that we should accept.

An alternative is not a solution that does not satisfy our interests, nor is it a solution that forces us to accommodate and let the other party have its way. An alternative gives us the ability to walk away from a potentially destructive conflict-resolution process with acceptance and caring. It gives us the ability to say, "Unless we can create a solution that benefits both of us, we should agree to disagree."

To illustrate the power of an alternative, let's return to the salary negotiation example from the previous chapter. As you recall, you want a raise from your present salary of $25,000 to a new salary of $30,000 because you have made significant contributions to your organization's objectives over the past eighteen months. You also know that other organizations are paying salaries ranging from $28,000 to $32,000 to people with your qualifications for the same type of work, so you are willing to take $28,000 as a bottom-line new salary. However, every time you approach your boss about this subject, she hesitates, claiming budget constraints and restrictive policies regarding salary increases. After some careful consideration, she finally offers you a new salary of $26,500—below your bottom line. What do you do?

Because you based the conflict resolution on a bottom line, you are not sure whether this offer satisfies your interests. Measuring an offer against a bottom line forces us into a competitive game, and any competitive interaction increases the chances of introducing destructive elements into conflict. For example, you might consider trying to enlist the support of human resources or your boss's boss, but you risk creating a new personal issue with your boss, who would feel backed into a corner or outmaneuvered. On the other hand, if you accept the offer, you may feel that you "lost" the conflict resolution because you did not achieve your positional demand of $28,000.

The problem in conflict resolution is not how to force a resolution that will produce an unsatisfying and destructive outcome. The problem is how to make sure that the collaborative resolution process produces an outcome that is based on mutual gain. If that cannot be accomplished, then we should seek alternatives that will satisfy our interests and needs. Prior to engaging in the resolution process, we need to establish an action plan in case we cannot reach a satisfactory agreement. That alternative serves as a better tool for evaluating the solutions that are created after we have understood the interests and examined the options.

In this example, you might establish an alternative of getting another job. You have to go beyond the possibility of another job; if you do not, you are not prepared to walk away from destructive interaction and you risk becoming attached as you try to force resolution. The more solidly your alternative satisfies your interests, the easier it is to stay detached responsibly throughout the interaction because you know that you are not dependent upon the other party. A possibility of a new job is only a possibility, whereas knowing that you have a new job helps you more objectively assess which solution best meets your criteria for resolution.

Suppose you receive an offer of $30,000 from an organization that is equivalent to your present employer in terms of benefits, culture, and management style. Now, when your current organization offers you $26,500, you can make an educated determination of which employer best satisfies your needs. If your boss decides to play hardball and not collaborate with you to understand your common interests and establish fair objective criteria for resolution, you can walk away without playing hardball in return and without sacrificing your principles of interaction. You can walk away from the interaction and say, "I appreciate the time you have taken to discuss these issues with me and try to establish some common ground. I wish you well in your efforts to find an employee who satisfies your interests." In other words, you can agree to disagree agreeably.

On the other hand, you may find out, for example, that despite your information about market rates, you could not obtain an offer higher than $26,000. Or, another organization might offer $32,000, but the management style and working conditions of the new company may not be to your liking. Or, you might not get an offer at all, leaving only the alternative of quitting your present job for something new or outside your current profession. If money is your primary interest, you also can stay in your present position and moonlight on the weekends. In all cases, you have alternatives. These alternatives may not satisfy your interests as well as continued employment with your present organization. However, establishing the alternative before the interaction with your current employer gives you a realistic standard of comparison when you examine the solutions.

When we try to collaborate without knowing our alternative, we are resolving in the dark. However, an accurate perception of reality helps us maintain the self-awareness and detached responsibility that lead to wise decisions. As the old saying goes, a bird in the hand is worth two in the bush. Understanding our alternatives prior to the resolution process provides the bird in the hand that empowers us to creatively explore the options for the two in the bush. Understanding the other party's alternatives to agreement with us will help us understand why that party needs us and is seeking an interdependent solution. It gives us a clearer picture of why the other party might stay engaged in the interaction.

Finding an alternative solution gives us the inner peace and confidence required to sustain application of our principles of interaction when uncooperative parties present challenges to collaboration. This is an extension of the philosophy of mutual gain because we communicate that if we cannot reach win-win solutions that mutually satisfy our interests, then we should not try to force an unsatisfactory resolution. It is better that we both fulfill our needs in other ways so that we can maintain a positive, constructive relationship with each other.

Third-Party Intervention

As discussed at the beginning of this chapter, there may be times during conflict when the parties cannot effectively apply the principles of Listening to Conflict. The interaction may be overwhelming to the disputants because of the significance of the personal issues involved in the disagreement. Mistrust and suspicion may cause competitive tactics to seep into the process and prevent either party from reducing the tensions of the exchange. Emotional minds may work in high gear and cause the rational minds to misperceive any attempts at collaboration as deceptive, phony, and destructive. In these situations, especially when the alternatives are not preferred, it may be wise to bring in a third party to help resolve the dispute.

Quarreling children call a parent to settle their disagreements. Employees appeal to their boss. Labor and management go to arbitration. Disconnecting spouses seek counseling to prevent going to court. We often look to an outside or higher authority to help us find answers that we could not envision on our own.

Third parties can improve the resolution process in a variety of ways. They may help us prepare for an interaction by acting as a sounding board as we think through the issues. They also may initiate the exchange by communicating more supportively the issues that need to be discussed. Third parties may help the disputants listen to one another by acting as an empathic translator. They are more detached from the conflict and are not clouded by any emotional investment. Therefore, they are in a better position to understand the underlying interests and needs that are misperceived and misinterpreted by the parties in heated conflict. Third parties also can help to identify criteria for solutions and can create and participate in a more effective brainstorming process that generates solutions leading to consensus decisions. In short, these outsiders can help us follow the steps of collaboration in order to produce constructive resolution.

There are four primary types of third-party intervention: litigation, arbitration, mediation, and experts. Each has both benefits and risks, but only two, mediation and experts, help produce collaborative resolution.

1. *Litigation.* Litigation is the process of going to court to achieve resolution. The third party, a judge or jury, listens to a presentation of positions by each side, then makes a ruling with regard to the outcome of a dispute. Litigation forces us into a competitive mode by casting the dispute around a single issue. It is costly to both parties and often produces outcomes that neither find satisfactory. It also can be more time-consuming than any other type of intervention. Litigation is especially destructive to relationships because it does not deal with any of the personal issues of the dispute. Consequently, while litigation

produces a clear winner and loser, both parties may leave court feeling empty or as if they have lost. The main benefit to litigation is that it creates a binding resolution to the objective issues of the conflict.

2. *Arbitration.* Like litigation, arbitration uses a third party to listen to the positions of each party and make a ruling as to the outcome of a dispute. Arbitrators may hear and rule on a single issue, or they may rule on multiple issues to create an overall settlement package. Arbitration also may be binding or voluntary. Under binding arbitration, the parties are required to comply with the decision, either by law or by their own previous commitment. Under voluntary arbitration, the parties present their positions to an arbitrator to get an opinion as to what will be a fair decision, but they are not required to comply with the decision. Finally, in a third approach to arbitration, the arbitrator selects one of the final offers made by the parties and does not create new solutions based on the information presented.

The advantage to arbitration is that it proposes a resolution to the dispute. It also ends the conflict faster than the prolonged process of a challenging and potentially destructive attempt at collaboration. The disadvantages of arbitration are many. First, if both parties know that they have the option of using an arbitrator, they may be less likely to make a disciplined effort to collaborate. Consequently, they may more easily fall into a destructive competitive mode of interaction. Another problem is that unless the arbitrated decision satisfies the interests of both parties, they are likely to perceive the process as unfair over the long term. Frequently, arbitration does not produce decisions based on mutual gain because the process focuses primarily on positions rather than on interests. Finally, since arbitration takes the parties out of the decision-making process, it is less likely that they will be committed to implementing the agreed-upon solution.

3. *Mediation.* Mediation is a process in which a third party enters the resolution process to help the parties make a decision, as opposed to rendering the decision. Unlike in litigation or arbitration, in mediation the third party has no formal power to impose its own decision. The first objective of a mediator is to facilitate a discussion of the issues. The mediator meets with the

parties separately and together to understand the interests and establish criteria for solutions. At the beginning stages of mediation, a mediator listens to the conflict in an attempt to facilitate the relationship between disputant and mediator and gain the parties' acceptance. Once this has been established, the mediator uses reflective responses, questions, and the steps of collaboration to translate, encourage, guide, and confirm understanding. Mediation can be either *facilitative* (or neutral) or *evaluative* (interjecting their own ideas for solution). Throughout the interaction, the mediator tries to establish a supportive and constructive environment.

In order for mediation to be effective, the parties must be willing to engage in collaboration through a neutral third party and have a stake in resolving the problem. In other words, the parties still must want to collaborate to reach mutual gain. If the disagreement has degenerated into an intensely competitive interaction, then the process is less likely to be effective. Another risk to mediation is the nonbinding nature of solutions. If one party becomes unsatisfied, or if the parties' constituencies exert competitive influence on the process, the mediated solution will break down. Mediation has become especially popular in employee relations and family disputes.

4. *Experts.* A final type of third-party intervention that can be interjected into the conflict-resolution process is expert information. The objective of neutral experts is to provide data, facts, and information that may help the parties improve their understanding of the objective issues in a dispute. Their role is not to understand the interests or develop solutions, but only to provide the expertise the parties need in order to interpret their interests and create objective criteria for solutions. The information may be technical in nature, or it may relate to understanding the process and standards of conflict resolution.

Challenges to Listening to Conflict

Whenever we are faced with a challenge to our principles of interaction and the Listening to Conflict approach, we are provided with a true test of our discipline, desire, and patience. Our biggest challenge will be the battle between the concern we have for our own needs and the concern we have for the other party's needs. If we lose sight of our desire for mutual gain, then we are likely to send conflicting signals to the other party that will increase that party's defensiveness and cause him or her to fall back into other orientations to conflict resolution. The following questions and answers illustrate the challenges we will face as we try to listen to conflict.

1. *I have tried, but no matter what I do, I cannot like or accept the other party. I cannot find anything redeemable about that party as a person or group. What do I do now?*

    We do not just dislike people. Our feelings about them originate somewhere. Something about their actions, attitude, idiosyncrasies, or social-cultural background causes us to perceive them as unacceptable.

    Hatred of oneself is inseparable from hatred, or dislike and lack of acceptance, of another. Acceptance requires that we first have enough self-awareness to understand why we do not like another person. We must assess the interpersonal zones that the other party has invaded and isolate the source of our discomfort. Initially, we may not know why we do not like the person, we only know that our intuition or emotional mind sends us signals that indicate a lack of acceptance. Review the exercises in Chapter 2, especially the questions about hot zones, and the questions under acceptance in Chapter 3 to begin to regain self-awareness.

    Once you are aware of the specific behavior that you find unacceptable, you can separate the person from the behavior. Maybe there are a number of behaviors that you find unsatisfactory, in which case you should isolate them all. Next, consider what is prompting the person to act that way. Try to identify what is going on in her or his conscious and subconscious emotional mind to create the behavior or situation. Seek to understand how the person feels, especially how he or she perceives you.

    A second strategy is to facilitate the relationship. The more time we spend with someone, the more likely it is that we will like him or her. Find a common interest, a shared hobby, or a mutual pursuit and build frequent interactions around that activity. Go to lunch or meet for coffee. Get to know the person outside of the context of the conflict.

Finally, if all else fails, detach responsibly and exercise your alternative solution. If you do not yet have an alternative, develop one. Some situations simply do not allow the possibility of collaborative behavior because the conditions for social order or mutual trust do not exist. If we do not like someone, and especially if we detest him or her, then we are in one of these situations. The only way we can avoid the trap of destructive, competitive behavior is to transform the interaction or leave the situation. If you have followed the Listening to Conflict approach to no avail, then create a solution that will prevent you from engaging in destructive interaction and violating your principles of interaction.

2. *What do I do if the other party does not want to collaborate? What if the other party chooses another orientation to conflict?*

When the other party sends you signals that it does not want to collaborate, it is time to listen empathically. Immerse yourself fully into this mode and listen deeply to understand *why* that party is resistant. What is the history of our relationship with the other party? Have we sent conflicting signals about our intent to collaborate? If so, then empathic listening demonstrates acceptance and a desire for mutual gain and will make sure that we understand the interests that we need to satisfy. When we convey our understanding of the other party's explicit and implicit meaning, this opens blocked communication channels and reveals that party's concerns and issues. As we demonstrate acceptance of these needs, we build a remarkable trust, and the other party is likely to ask for our thoughts, ideas, feelings, and opinions.

When the other party does not have the skills to collaborate, we can help by listening empathically. We can help the party sort through personal issues and identify unconscious emotions that are blocking collaboration. We can also help to untangle the personal issues from the objective issues in the dispute to reveal the other party's core needs. This will help us shift that party's competitive, positional focus to an interest-based, collaborative approach.

A common theme of those who do not like to collaborate is a lack of confidence and self-esteem. At times, this may be difficult to see or believe because the defense mechanisms that these people have developed over the years may demonstrate anything but a lack of confidence. Listen empathically, however, and you will see hurt, fearful people who need our help to collaborate. Since we are self-aware and have mastered the principles of interaction, we can provide the assistance they need in order to shift from their destructive strategies to constructive collaboration.

Finally, if all else fails, call in a third party or exercise your alternative solution.

If the other party is competitive:

A competitor typically will enter the conflict-resolution process with a firm position, and our reaction is often to immediately attack this position or to defend ourselves by stating our opposite position. As soon as we do this, we have established a competitive game in which the outcome will be based on obtaining as much of the original demand as we are able to.

We must resist the temptation to enter the attack-and-defend game. Instead, we should jump into an empathic listening mode and try to understand the interests behind the other party's position. We shift competitors away from their game and help them to understand their own needs and concerns. As they communicate deeper levels of their needs, we can reframe their positions as interests they have in common with us or as problems to be solved rather than demands to be met.

One risk, however, is that while a collaborative approach usually makes collaborators behave even more collaboratively, it can have the exact opposite effect on competitors—it can make them even more competitive and resistant than before. In response to this, demonstrate acceptance and welcome their criticism and personal attacks, emotional ploys, attempts to manipulate data and facts, and deception. Our ability to remain detached responsibly will inoculate us against their assault and keep us focused on mutual gain.

Finally, competitors compete to feel better about themselves. Often we perceive competitors as having large egos. The opposite, in fact, is true. Ultra competitors do not have strong self-concepts, or their self-concepts are tied substantially to competing. How many times have we seen professional athletes come out of retirement because they need the self-esteem boost from competing? Our response to competitors should never be to compete in return because when we do so, we challenge their self-concept. This only increases their desire to reaffirm themselves through additional competing. The best thing we can do is boost their self-esteem by demonstrating acceptance of *them*, facilitating a relationship with *them*, and listening to understand *them*. Then, with our understanding of the interests, we can link their interests to ours and reframe their position as a common problem to be solved.

If the other party avoids conflict:

Parties who avoid conflict often appear indifferent to the interaction. They neither push their own objectives nor show concern for the other's objectives. In reality, avoiders are afraid of conflict. It is overwhelming to their emotional mind. If we want to get avoiders to collaborate, we need to create a low-key, safe environment in which they can discuss the issues at their own pace. We listen empathically, but we should respond by repeating or rephrasing rather than reflecting. The active listening responses are more effective during the early stages of the interaction because they do not go as deep emotionally. Repeating and rephrasing let avoiders gradually enter the resolution process.

It also is important that we create conversational space by using silence. Avoiders frequently are introverted and therefore may need more time to think through what they want to say before articulating. A comfortable silence demonstrates acceptance of their interpersonal zones and personal style. We also should help avoiders reframe their criticism of us as well as of themselves. By welcoming their comments, we demonstrate trust and open them up to collaboration.

If the other party accommodates:

People who accommodate generally have low self-esteem. They often use solving your problems as a way to feel better about themselves. In the process, they neglect to take care of themselves and their needs. Over the long term, however, resentment builds, and there is often a breakdown in their relationships with us or in their own emotional health.

To convert accommodators into collaborators, we must make an extra effort to listen to their needs. Be careful, because as soon as you start to make progress in identifying their issues and interests, they will turn the tables and try to help *you.* Accommodators are often uncomfortable *receiving* from others. We must draw out their needs and spend additional time confirming their feelings and thoughts. When we examine the options for solution, we should ask them, "How do you feel about that?" or "What are your thoughts for . . . ?" Encouraging, almost forcing, their involvement and help in satisfying their own interests will prevent problems down the road. We may even have to insist that we will not let them satisfy our needs unless they let us help them.

If the other party does not want to collaborate, the process of converting him or her can take time. We cannot resolve the underlying personal issues that interfere with collaboration in five or ten minutes of interaction. Time allows us to facilitate the relationship, to build trust, and to bring down the walls preventing collaboration.

3. *What do I do if I do not have the time to collaborate?*

If you do not have the time to collaborate, then exercise your alternative or invite third-party intervention. You could consider another strategy, such as competing, accommodating, or avoiding, but you would not be sticking to your principles of interaction, and you would confirm in the other's mind that you really did not want to collaborate in the first place. A noncollaborative strategy will work only if you have facilitated a solid relationship with the other party. Although you are still sending mixed signals, the other party might let you off the hook this time as long as the next interaction is collaborative.

If we are starting from ground zero in the interaction with

the other party, time pressures make collaboration challenging. It takes time to facilitate the relationship and understood the interests. However, if you have a long-standing relationship with another party, a new conflict can be more quickly resolved using collaboration because collaboration has become second nature for both of you.

If you know up front that time will be a factor that limits your ability to collaborate, then establish a good alternative. That way, when you run out of time, you can achieve mutual gain and maintain the relationship by not forcing either of you to accept a less than satisfactory solution.

4. *But my boss or another third party tells me I have to have an agreement with this person . . . and soon.*

It sounds as if you have a second conflict to resolve. You can use the same skills on your boss that you use in your principled interactions with others.

Collaborative conflict resolution seeks to obtain the best agreement possible for both parties. We risk an unwise and unsatisfactory resolution when we place time limits on the interaction and prevent both parties from proceeding through the stages of collaborative resolution. We also nibble away at our efforts to facilitate a relationship that will maintain the constructive environment. If we truly have time limits, we also should develop strong alternative solutions. Then, if we cannot achieve mutual gain before the time limit, we can exercise our alternative and maintain the otherwise effective, collaborative relationship.

5. *My boss does not want to collaborate, either.*

See the response to question 2. You might also exercise your alternative. It will be difficult to remain detached responsibly and demonstrate acceptance while working in an environment that does not value the Listening to Conflict principles of collaborative mutual gain. It is possible, but it will take an extraordinary amount of discipline, desire, and patience.

6. *What if I do not have power in the relationship?*

Power is mostly a matter of perception. To prove this, why would someone with absolute power bother to engage in conflict resolution with us? If someone really had absolute power, that person could dictate what he or she wanted from us without our involvement. Therefore, the fact that another party engages in the resolution process suggests that we have something that party needs. When we determine the nature of the need, we more fully understand our interdependence with that party.

On the other hand, sometimes the other party really does have more power. Typically, those with more power eventually dominate, or compete, to get their way. Rather than accommodating or engaging in destructive behavior, our best strategy is to strengthen our alternative solution. The stronger our alternative, the easier it will be to walk away amicably before we lose control and engage in destructive behaviors.

For example, suppose you were having a conflict over rates with your utility company, an organization that is often perceived to have power over us (no pun intended). Most of us would assume that either we accommodate and pay what the company asks, or we do not have electricity. However, what alternatives do we have if the conflict resolution breaks down? We could switch to solar power, or install our own generator in the backyard. We might also decide to use candles and batteries. In other words, we have alternatives that would let us walk away from the destructive interaction with the company if it played the power card, a competitive tool. The alternatives may not always be preferable, but they are nonetheless alternatives that allow us to satisfy our interests independent of the other party. By strengthening our alternative, we level the playing field of our interaction.

7. *What if there is nothing to listen to? What if the other party doesn't seem to want to talk?*

There are a variety of reasons why people are hesitant to open up and communicate. They may have a social zone that is inclined toward introversion, or they may be avoiders. Whatever the reason, we need to create an environment that draws out their thoughts, needs, and interests.

As a first step, use silence. Silence can give someone the emotional space to work through thoughts and emotions before articulating. Silence also creates a healthy tension in the interaction that will make one or both of us want to break the dead air. Maintain discipline, desire, and patience and wait for the other party to speak first. Then immediately enter the listening mode to understand the interests. You might consider responding less frequently so that the other party does not have an excuse to stop talking. You might also consider facilitating the relationship and identifying less emotional items to discuss.

Another technique to get the other party to open up is to ask an open-ended question (see question 14). This will create enough conversation to allow us to jump into the empathic listening mode. The process of drawing out a silent, noncommunicative person takes time, but it will build trust to improve interaction and get the person's involvement in collaboration.

8. *What do we do if we feel threatened or abused, or if we are fearful of the interaction?*

People who threaten, intimidate, and abuse usually have incredibly low self-esteem. They are in immense psychological pain. They are hurting and fearful. That said, if the interaction exposes you to physical harm, *leave.* Exercise an alternative solution, call in a third party, but do not stick around for the abuse. Do not accommodate, although you might accommodate in the short term to buy time to abandon the situation. For example, do you collaborate with a mugger? No, you accommodate in the short term by giving the mugger your wallet or purse, which buys you time to call the police (third-party intervention) or run like mad (alternative).

The accommodation is not as much about satisfying the other party's needs as it is about self-preservation.

9. *How do I get out of an agreement?*

Getting out of an agreement is tricky business because it does not demonstrate the principle of fair play, at least on the surface. Therefore, when you initiate the exchange and confront the other party, you need to have solid data that suggest that the agreement is not meeting your interests (or the other party's interests). Objective, measurable data and facts will reestablish the sense of fair play that is required to achieve collaborative solutions.

If the other party objects to your reopening the conflict resolution, demonstrate acceptance, because from that party's perspective you are being unfair. Then, listen to understand the interests that will not be satisfied if you change the conditions of the agreement. Reframe these interests as an opportunity for you to collaborate to produce an even better agreement than before. If you want to walk away completely and exercise an alternative solution, then help the other party to identify ways to satisfy its interests. It is the least you can do!

10. *How do I break a deadlock?*

A deadlock is a sign that we are behaving positionally. One of the tasks of collaboration is to go beyond positions and listen to the underlying interests and needs. Therefore, when you are faced with a deadlock, the first step is to concentrate more fully on listening to understand the other party. Other methods for breaking deadlocks are as follows:

- Review the agreement and discuss it to ensure mutual understanding.
- Emphasize mutual interests.
- Reevaluate the criteria for solutions.
- Take a time-out to create emotional space to consider and discuss the agreement.
- Facilitate the relationship by discussing everything but the conflict.
- Change the meeting location.
- Call in an expert to assess the objective information and solutions.
- Discuss "what-if" scenarios.
- Agree to implement a solution on a trial basis.
- Be patient.

11. *How can I establish credibility and trust?*

Trust is an important ingredient of constructive, collaborative relationships. However, trust is a matter of choice. Either the other party chooses to trust us or it does not. Sometimes, no matter how sincerely our actions demonstrate the principles of interaction and a desire for mutual gain, the other party's past experiences and emotional memories may prevent that party from trusting us.

To make sure you are behaving in ways that are trustworthy, you should also exhibit the following characteristics:

- *Courtesy.* Respect the other party's time and position. Eliminate distractions and interruptions.
- *Composure.* Maintain self-awareness and self-mastery.
- *Sincerity.* Mean what you say. Demonstrate acceptance.
- *Integrity.* Seek mutual gain. Speak positively about that party and others. Admit your weaknesses and mistakes.
- *Fairness.* Use objective data, facts, and information. Base decisions on sound reasoning.
- *Reliability.* Follow through on your commitments. Pay attention to details.
- *Competence.* Prepare. Do your homework. Know your facts.

12. *How do we know we are not being duped, or ripped off, by the other party?*

If you do your homework during the preparation phase and you have a solid alternative, then you will have the information you need in order to determine whether you have arrived at a wise resolution. As long as the solution satisfies all our interests, it does not matter whether the other party has ripped us off. In fact, maybe we satisfied an important personal need and boosted the other party's self-esteem in the process. However, the solution must satisfy us over both the short and the long term. If the other party goes back on its word and does not live up to its end of the agreement, then you will know that something is going on. You will have to initiate the exchange, listen, and understand the interests in order to find out why the other party did not follow through with the commitment.

13. *I am having a huge personal conflict with a family member, and I cannot identify any alternative solutions. What do I do?*

The closer we are to people emotionally, the more likely it is that when our conflicts go bad, they go really bad. Usually, the conflict starts as a small disagreement—for example, a family member did not call to let us know that he was going to be an hour late. We have a few negative words about it, such as, "Why didn't you call? I was worried sick. . . . You should've called. . . . Dinner is ruined." The family member says, "I'm sorry," or "I dunno. I just didn't think about it," or some other variation, and the issue is dropped.

What happened in that small interaction, however, was that both sides started keeping score. We feel resentful because his response did not satisfy our emotional needs (fear that something had happened to him, hurt that he did not consider our feelings, etc.) He feels resentful because although subconsciously he knows he should have called, the way we confronted him put him on the defensive. It embarrassed him, and he had to save face and protect his self-concept.

A couple of weeks later, something else occurs. Then one day later, another incident happens. And so on, and so on, until . . . now, we have a *huge* conflict with this person. We did not manage the small conflicts effectively, if we managed them at all, and they are all tangled into a great big mess. We do not know where to begin to resolve the conflict, and we certainly cannot identify any alternative solutions that are satisfactory. If the other person involved is a spouse, we do not want a divorce. If it is a child, we do not want to kick her out of the house. We are attached and gradually turning competitive. We want this person to behave differently. We *wish . . . if only . . .* he *should.*

The first thing we must do is to detach responsibly by preparing for the interaction. Take another look at the conflict as a whole, then break it into all of its component parts. In some cases, this is hard to do because there are 50 million little conflicts that we have not dealt with. In those cases, try to isolate the most important *objective* issues and deal with them *one at a time.* As long as we bundle the component conflicts into one big issue, we will not be able to detach and resolve.

Another place to start is by completing the exercises in Chapter 3 designed to help us accept the family member. Hopefully, we can find things that we like about him or her that will help us separate the person from the behavior. Once we do that, we will be better able to deconstruct the conflict into smaller bite-sized pieces. Once the conflict is of manageable size, we can slowly, and with great discipline, desire, and patience, begin to collaborate toward mutual gain.

14. *How can we use questions and demonstrate the principles of interaction?*

We have not talked about questions so far because they come more naturally to us. We are trained through our developmental processes and education to be analytical and evaluative. Therefore, questions are likely to be a part of our everyday repertoire. However, if questions are going to be used as a tool of Listening to Conflict, they must demonstrate a consistency with our principles of interaction. The key is to shift from asking in an attacking mode to asking supportively. We need to ask questions in such a way as to demonstrate consistency of acceptance and a desire to understand.

While preparing for the interaction and initiating the exchange, we can use questions to confront the other party; while facilitating the interaction and understanding the interests, we can use questions to build the relationship and to clarify information the other party has communicated. We can also use questions to gather information that is important for our understanding and to help us identify the other party's underlying reasons or motives. While examining the solutions and reaching consensus, we can use questions to examine solutions, to provide criteria for solutions, and to reframe the other party's positions.

Remember that asking questions is *not* listening and is best not included as a primary strategy for understanding the interests. It may give the impression that we are pretending to listen or that we are listening in order to evaluate or judge. On the other hand, questions may be just the thing to help draw out a silent collaborator or give a competitor pause to think. As a rule, questions should be left to the problem-solving stages of resolution.

There are two primary types of question. A *closed-ended* question, such as, "Did you like the weather yesterday?" produces a yes or no answer or can be answered in one or two words. This style of questioning often makes the other party feel as if he or she is on the witness stand being cornered by an opposing attorney. An *open-ended* question, on the other hand, asks for a response that is filled with information. For example, "What are your ideas about . . . ?" is an open-ended question that should produce more than a few words. Open-ended questions are often a way to get the conversation started so that we can jump into the empathic listening mode.

Generally, we need to make sure that our questions do not put the other party on the defensive. They must sound supportive, interested, and encouraging. The following list should provide you with some examples to get you started.

Build the relationship	*"What are your thoughts about . . . ?"*
	"I'd like to hear your opinion."
	"What can I do to help?"
Gather information	*"Please tell me more about . . ."*
	"What are your thoughts about . . . ?"
	"What are your priorities?"
	"What if . . . ?"
Clarify information	*"What did you mean by . . . ?"*
	"Could you give me an example of . . . ?"
	"Help me understand . . ."
Identify interests	*"Why . . . ?"*
	"Help me understand why . . ."
	"What's your reasoning behind . . ."
Provide information	*"Did you know that . . . ?"*
	"Help me understand the difference between my information, which says . . . , and your information, which says . . ."
	"What if . . . ?"
Probe for solutions	*"How can we . . . ?"*
	"What would you do . . . ?"
	"What if . . . ?"
	"If you could . . . ?"

Reframe positions	*"It sounds as if you are saying . . ."* *"What would you do if you were in my shoes?"* *"How does that relate to . . . ?"*
Confront and initiate	*"I'm feeling . . . What are your thoughts about . . . ?"* *"You seem . . . Am I understanding correctly?"* *"I'm not sure what to do about . . . What are your thoughts?"*

7

Cultures of Constructive Conflict

The fastest way to learn is to discover a person or group which reaches totally different conclusions to your own when looking at the same reality.

Robert Theobald

If civilization is to survive, we must cultivate the science of human relationships—the ability of all peoples, of all kinds, to live together, in the same world at peace.

Franklin Delano Roosevelt

At least once every generation, organizations undergo fundamental changes in the way they conduct themselves. New technologies, different models of governance, and increased competition, for example, alter the demands placed on the quality and focus of interactions. These demands compel organizations to change continuously to cope with the new and more challenging environment, but the pressures of change increase the risk of destructive discord. This is true whether the organization is a government, a corporation, a nonprofit agency, a school system, a social-cultural group, or a family. However, as the speed of change increases and the complexity of issues expand, what is required is not changes in the techniques that produce essential outcomes, but changes in the underlying assumptions on which we base our model of behavior and the resulting approach to managing and resolving conflict.

Sometime around the late 1960s, we entered an era in which large, dominant empires began to systematically deconstruct themselves into smaller, more focused enterprises. Governments decolonized (the Soviet Union being a recent example of this), companies began shedding nonessential divisions, and families decreased in size and spread out across diverse geographical regions. The era of the "great" and centralized society has given way to a period of interest-driven, anti-institutional sentiment. Mass marketing is gone in favor of micromarketing, and homogeneity has been replaced by diversity.

Correspondingly, the shift from the industrial era to the information age has altered the nature of the workplace. Industrial-era workers were employed for a lifetime by large organizations. They worked their shift on the assembly line under close supervision, and were expected to be loyal, obedient, and subservient to the greater interest of the whole. In contrast, information-age knowledge workers are contingent or temporary employees, consultants or subcontractors, or a "just-in-time work force—fluid, flexible, disposable" (Morrow, 1993). They work for themselves or are part of relatively unsupervised, empowered, or self-directed work teams. They are expected to learn quickly, add value, and change rapidly.

While the organization model based on hierarchy, structure, and predictability is collapsing, this new mode of interaction is not yet fully understood. Consequently, the transformation has caused considerable destructive conflict in all aspects of life as individuals fight to retain their competitive niche, or their comfort zones of existence. They continue to apply the old rules to the new reality. They continue to compete for their piece of the distributed pie, but the competitive model proves self-defeating as the lines fade between competitor and partner, subordinate and equal.

The composition and rules for the new organization model are not yet known, but there are elements of both current changes and predictions of the future that do seem consistent. These factors have begun to define our social reality and the corresponding challenges for maintaining cultures of constructive conflict.

• *Pluralism.* Unfortunately, diversity has become a cliché in our cultural landscape. We can hardly read a professional publication or attend a trade conference without hearing of the concepts and challenges of the diverse ethnic, racial, religious, and social groups that participate in our organizations. Statistical studies have demonstrated that there have been significant changes in the social-demographic composition of the workforce and other social institutions. However, the real change has occurred not in the composition of our organizations, but in the character of participation. Rather than assimilating into the homogeneous mix, each group has maintained an autonomous participation in and development of its traditional culture or special interest and therefore has developed a powerful political voice.

The result is that we have a mass culture defined by its distinct parts, resulting in more than one definition of the social reality. Each group has its own set of narrowly focused objectives that establish its independent existence within the confines of the larger society. At the same time, each group's objectives also establish a necessary interdependence with other groups in the social structure. In other words, we have a desire for independence combined with a necessary dependence on other specialized providers of goods or services. Each group is simultaneously self-sufficient and non-self-sufficient. The groups must be interdependent.

This poses especially interesting challenges for managing and resolving conflict. Social-cultural influences and the resulting forces driving our need for affiliation shape many of our perceptions of reality. Correspondingly, these perceptions are lodged in our minds as powerful emotional memories that are then reinforced and supported by further affiliation. If the perceptions, resulting memories, and reinforcement are negative, then a defensive and protective reaction is established against the perceived individual, group, or social situation. Therefore, while one version of social reality necessitates interdependence, another version resents the dependence of the forced interaction, further intensifying competitive orientations.

• *Globalization.* Another consistent theme discussed widely in the popular press is the notion of the global economy. It is indeed a reality, but it is shaped by more than the trade of goods and services across borders. Nations' economies are no longer isolated from the impact of international markets because the international economy is interconnected through the flow of information, money, goods, and services. A financial crisis in the Far East has a direct impact on the economies of the United States, Latin America, and Europe. In addition, traditional factors of production such as natural resources, land, and production capacity are not as important for competitiveness as are information and knowledge.

It is clear that our interdependence is increasing. Economic policy is shaped less by free trade or protectionism and more by reciprocity and mutual gain. National and regional boundaries are disappearing, and it is difficult to determine the nationality of corporations as their operations become geographically distributed. While distinct national and regional markets still exist, the market is increasingly defined as a world market in which no one country or organization maintains a commanding competitive edge. The economic data also suggest that while developing economies have begun to flourish, it has not been at the expense of more established economies.

The old model, based on an attitude of limits, embodied high levels of competition, protectionism, and nationalism, and suggested that natural resources, technology, information, and capital were limited commodities. But the existing reality suggests that while there may be a limited quantity of a specific resource (say, for example, coal), there is, in fact, an abundance of resources that satisfy the same interest (energy sources). In addition, the fading boundaries and increased "competition" did not necessarily create a true competitive effect. One organization did not lose because of the emergence of another. It lost because it could not adapt to the changing environment. The only limited resource seems to be human intellectual capital.

• *Information.* With the advent of the knowledge age has come the rise of information as the primary asset of the modern organization. The proliferation of information has reduced the need for hierarchical communication structures and increased the numbers of knowledge-based specialists within organizations. However, the knowledge worker is typically more resistant to command and control systems than the industrial worker, and has directly confronted the need for the traditional distribution of power within an organization hierarchy. Flatter organization structures and self-directed work teams are examples of this effect.

Information is causing a similar shift of power at the organizational level. A small, upstart software company can have market power equal to that of IBM, if not greater, for example, within a relatively short period of time. Its information can create advantages of technology or innovation and allow it to serve more specific segments of the market. Information has changed the balance of power both internally and externally.

The traditional organization model devalues human assets by imposing strict mechanization and procedures, and suggests that if the organization is faced with a situation that requires protection of capital assets, human assets are expendable. Under this assumption, humans are factors of production. However, current labor shortages, combined with educational efforts that cannot keep pace with increasing knowledge requirements, should cause organizations to reconsider their attitude toward human capital. While a new relationship has not yet been defined, it must consider a process of sustaining more constructive interaction.

The Impact on Conflict Management

The clash of the old and new models is increasing conflict within and across our organizations. But at the same time, it is also redefining how we have to manage, and ultimately resolve, conflict in the new environment. The competitive bargaining model called for a structured distribution of limited resources of information, power, and capital based on various competitors' success at using the model to gain advantage. Those individuals, organizations, and nations that were better at competing controlled the pie, and those who applied the model ineffectively were cut off from participation and received the crumbs.

Success in the new reality, however, is linked more strongly than ever to our ability to recognize our interdependence and achieve constructive collaborative solutions. It also is linked powerfully to human effort and knowledge rather than to format, systems, or structure. Therefore, the paradigm based on competitive victory is hard to maintain because market competitors become business partners, employees become future co-workers, and dependent workers become knowledge specialists on whom we depend.

While the requirements for success are changing, our organization and individual structure and style have not. Thus far, our response as organizations and individuals all too frequently has been to create a variety of "programs" designed to change the *techniques* of work without changing the principles of interaction. This explains why we have cycled through an infinite number of management fads that have had few, if any, long-term results. For organizational change to be sustained, a change of consciousness must take place. For a *culture* to change, not only must the systems and processes that define the social group change, but this must be accompanied by a corresponding change within the individual. No organizational transformation will be successful without both events.

Most organization change efforts begin by trying to drive a program from top levels down, and from organization doctrine to individual value. However, as we have discussed in preceding chapters, collaborative conflict resolution must be a principle of interaction supported by individual self-awareness and self-mastery. The principles of interaction are ineffective as a technique or system because our natural competitive orientation is subtly revealed through our half-hearted attempts to collaborate. This sends conflicting messages to other parties that will erode the trust required for a free flow of information. Therefore, a culture that supports constructive, collaborative conflict resolution must be built upon guiding principles of interaction and supported by systems and structures that reinforce, support, and ultimately compel individual change.

Organization Requirements

Internal systems that support the Listening to Conflict principles may include different steps and procedures that uniquely represent the individual characteristics of each social structure, such as organizations, schools, groups, and families. However, all organization systems should share a common set of objectives founded upon the principles required for individual application of constructive conflict resolution. These requirements will serve to reinforce the development of internalized principles and to prevent destructive disputes and guide the process of collaborative resolution.

• *Shared perception of reality.* The challenges of our changing environment require the formation of alliances built around shared perceptions of reality. We must evolve beyond the separate factions of employee and management, supplier and customer, competitor and competitor, leader and led. These divisions often show up as hostilities, or at least as perceptions molded by different sets of assumptions, and create divisive personal issues that increase the incidence of competition and destructive interaction.

By building and strengthening shared realities, we create new affiliations that facilitate relationships and increase understanding of individual interests. The result is a shift from "us versus them" resistance and competition to collaborative efforts based on acceptance of unique individual contributions within the common collective. Building a shared perception requires frequent interaction, a free exchange of information, distinct objectives, and common sets and levels of competency.

Organizations that implement the philosophy of open-book management, for example, provide effective models for both the results of a shared perception of reality and the challenges encountered. The practice requires that every employee see and understand the company's financials, along with other information that is critical for tracking business performance. There are no secrets, no hierarchical dissemination of data, and no hidden motives. Employees have a direct stake in the outcomes and must develop skills that help create desired results. Representatives from organizations that practice open-book management frequently say that the open-book philosophy is the key to their *competitive* advantage. In reality, the key to their *effectiveness* is collaboration.

• *Operating agreements.* Operating agreements are more formal, or structural, requirements of cultures of constructive conflict resolution. They should identify clearly the results required in order to achieve mutual gain and the objective, measurable criteria that will be used to assess accomplishment. In addition, they should characterize the requisite policies, standards, and resources and the timing of evaluation.

These contracts are reciprocal communication tools consistent with the vanishing hierarchies and changing knowledge structures that necessitate, if not demand, collaborative partnerships. They establish the interdependent accountabilities required for mutual gain, and they help relationships evolve from employer–employee to partner–partner, from teacher–student to scholar–scholar, and even from parent–child to family contributor–family contributor.

Organizationally, this represents a shift away from traditional appraisal and evaluation systems that artificially place the power to assess in hands other than those of the object of the assessment. It also proposes that performance not be evaluated separately from commonly identified operating indicators. Instead, operating agreements require a shift from subjective standards to objective measures that drive collaborative accountability.

The 360-degree appraisal system is a step in the right direction, but it has limitations. In most cases, it still does not create a review of the "contract" of employment. Like most appraisal systems, it has as its focus the employee rather than the collaborative relationship between employee and organization. Collaborative operating agreements, in contrast, evaluate the interdependent relationship.

• *Clarified roles and accountabilities.* For operating agreements to foster collaborative success, organizations, families, and social groups must clearly establish the results expected of each interdependent contributor. However, the roles, responsibilities, and knowledge required to achieve the desired results should not be defined along lines of authority and command. Instead, they should be driven by desired outcomes, communication requirements, resource conditions, and expertise needed.

Self-directed work teams, for example, have demonstrated remarkable success when structured according to this approach. The teams are often task- or process-focused, with roles determined by task accountabilities, expertise, and required communication. Clarified roles and accountabilities, in effect, represent an application of detached responsibility to the organization in that distinct accountabilities allow individuals to concentrate on delivering individual results independently (detachment), while simultaneously contributing to organization results interdependently (responsibility).

• *Consensus decisions.* An organization, family, or social group cannot have a constructive collaborative environment without consensus decision making. This does not necessarily mean that every decision is made by consensus. Some decisions will be made on the basis of organization role or along lines of accountability. However, decisions that affect more than one individual or expert area must nurture interdependence by requiring participation and involvement. The consensus-building process manages the emotional elements, the personal issues, that were ignored under the old model, but are essential if the collaborative model is to be effective. If an employee is no longer an "employee," but an uncommitted, nonloyal, disenfranchised, virtual information provider, then consensus decisions are the only way to build the necessary commitment to success.

• *Conflict-resolution process.* The first four requirements for application of the Listening to Conflict approach by an organization represent the primary system elements that reinforce the principles of interaction. Nonetheless, the organization may need a secondary reinforcement structure to contain the resistance to and failure of any collaborative system that is established. This is especially true during periods of transition. A formalized conflict-resolution process based on the six steps of collaboration serves as a code to guide behavior and provides an alternative third-party process for mediating constructive resolution.

Any formal conflict-resolution process must seek to transform the dispute in an enduring manner, not just end the disagreement or suppress differing needs and expectations.

Accordingly, it must focus on prevention and reduction, rather than management and containment. The process also must support basic human needs and build shared perceptions of reality, while developing a variety of methods to address the diversity of issues and individual styles of interaction.

A conflict-resolution process must be more than a complaint system, since relatively few disputes find their way into the formal channels established in organizations because of employee fear of negative consequences. The process should confront conflicts in their entirety rather than simply isolating the interaction to individuals who lodge specific complaints. Constructive conflict-resolution processes recognize the collective nature of disputes and listen to understand the interests that represent the whole problem before examining the solutions for agreement.

The Effects of Training

Maintaining the right type and amount of conflict in an organization is critical to its success. As we have discussed, conflict centered on personal issues typically leads to negative emotions and destructive reactions that are detrimental to effective functioning. In contrast, conflict centered on objective issues, especially performance, survival, and development, can have remarkably positive effects on performance (Sessa, 1996). Since conflict is an important part of team success and interdependent collaboration is a requirement of the new social reality, creating an environment that supports constructive conflict management and resolution is essential.

Numerous studies have indicated that training individuals in collaborative conflict-resolution skills significantly improves their ability to manage and resolve conflict constructively (Stevahn, Johnson, Johnson, and Real, 1996; Ikemi and Kubota, 1996). Training in collaborative resolution improves the ability to listen and respond more empathically as well as to choose a collaborative orientation over a competitive orientation. In addition, individuals exposed to constructive conflict training acquire more positive attitudes toward conflict than those who do not receive training. The results from training have been demonstrated across all ages, social-cultural groups, and professional levels. Training results also have been similar for individuals and families.

The training environment itself is also critical to reinforcement of the skills. Collaborative learning rather than competitive or individualistic learning helps individuals achieve higher levels of retention, reasoning, internal motivation, and achievement. It also helps participants develop relationships that are more positive and leads to greater psychological health, self-esteem, and social competence.

It is apparent, however, that knowledge of collaborative methods, while important, is not enough to sustain a culture of constructive conflict resolution. Training must go beyond conveying ideas; it must actively and personally build experience with the multiple skills involved and provide ample feedback about performance. In addition, the environment, its systems, and its procedures must not interfere with the application of collaboration if the skills are to be integrated and sustained across all social interaction.

Constructive Conflict Training Requirements

Constructive conflict training, and in particular the Listening to Conflict skills, requires both an organization and an individual focus. In other words, training should introduce concepts to help individuals interact according to the standards of the organization, but it should also improve competencies at a more personal level. As previously noted, individual self-development is crucial if the principles are to take hold in the context of the larger organization, as are the frequency and practicality or reinforcement methods. In addition, to maintain a consistent culture, organizations should consider training longer-term contingent workers, suppliers, customers, and others who share interdependence. The following outlines the requirements for a successful collaborative training effort.

1. *Include constructive conflict-management education as part of the ongoing core curriculum.* Whether in corporations, schools,

nonprofit organizations, or families, we must educate, train, and develop individuals in the components of collaborative conflict resolution. This needs to be a process that builds upon the core individual skills and integrates them into the organizational context. The process also must be ongoing and repeated to transform technique into habit, concept into principle. In addition, training should incorporate role-plays, examples, and discussion centered on the participants' own experience so that concepts become practical and adapted to the participants' unique situations.

2. *Design programs around specific components of constructive collaboration.* Training in constructive conflict-management skills, particularly listening skills, should be broken into components that address different competencies and developmental stages. Pretraining and ongoing assessment of participants will assure that foundational elements are acquired and that participants are ready for increased levels of competency.

The core components of constructive collaboration training are:

- *Self-awareness.* Understanding yourself and recognizing your thoughts and feelings. Learning your interpersonal zones and capabilities. Making the connection to your behavior and reactions.
- *Emotional expression.* Understanding how to communicate your feelings and emotions both verbally and nonverbally to others in a constructive manner.
- *Managing emotions.* Developing the ability to modify emotional states and regulate feelings.
- *Stress management.* Making the connection between the mental and the physical. Learning how to monitor and regulate stress levels
- *Assertiveness.* Communicating your needs and concerns in a nonthreatening, nonemotional manner. Learning how to confront.
- *Perspective taking.* Seeing the world through the eyes of another person. Acquiring an "as if" mode of interaction.
- *Listening.* Learning to listen at levels 5 and 6. Understanding and implementing response techniques.

- *Questioning.* Asking questions supportively. Asking questions to evaluate and assess.
- *Creativity.* Developing abilities to experiment, associate, and innovate.
- *Problem solving.* Understanding objectives. Assessing and evaluating information. Diagnosing problems. Analyzing data.
- *Decision making.* Understanding how to compare information. Establishing criteria. Arriving at conclusions.
- *Group dynamics.* Learning team process and cooperation. Understanding and assigning roles and responsibilities.
- *Collaborative conflict resolution.* Understanding interests. Going beyond positions. Implementing the steps of conflict resolution. Applying the skills toward the practice of mediation.

3. *Design programs that are relevant to a variety of social-cultural factors and that take into account current levels of competency.* Training must take into account gender, race, ethnicity, religion, nationality, age, educational background, socioeconomic status, disability status, sexual orientation, and a host of other such social-cultural factors. These elements account for differing perceptions, interpersonal zones, and styles of managing conflict. In addition, training must take into account different levels of emotional and cognitive development.

Conflict-resolution training must go beyond changes in perceptions and attitudes to become a dialogue that recognizes existing pluralism, but that builds more established interdependence. Where groups are isolated because of geographic, occupational, or historical boundaries, training efforts must initiate and encourage interaction.

4. *Training environments should create conceptual conflict, controversy, and uncertainty.* Instructors and instruction should not only convey the relevant concepts and skills of constructive conflict but also model the behavior. When the learning environment creates an atmosphere of constructive controversy, participants more rapidly grasp the principles of collaborative resolution. Individuals who engage in controlled controversy

have been shown to be more motivated to know others' opinions and to develop an understanding and appreciation of them. In addition, training participants who are exposed to controversial discussions develop a more accurate understanding of others than do participants in safe, harmonious environments (Tjosvold and Johnson, 1977).

Challenges to the organizational core should be encouraged because the divergent opinion and resulting debate creates intellectual and emotional curiosity—an important first step in the development of listening and understanding skills. The environment also is beneficial because it more adequately prepares training participants to manage the stress of all aspects of organizational change.

5. *Teach direct conflict management and resolution and also mediation skills.* Individuals will be called upon not only to demonstrate the principles and skills of constructive conflict in their own interactions, but also to act as models and reinforcing agents for others. The skills of mediation are quite similar to those of constructive conflict management in terms of establishing a listening-based, interest-focused environment and a collaborative problem-solving attitude. The additional skills required for mediation include facilitating group process, directive confrontation, and using questions as a tool to focus and guide the interaction. The development of mediation skills across various sections of the organization should serve to reinforce, encourage, and assist collaborative interaction.

6. *Train those who implement and sustain the effort.* The final element required for implementation of the Listening to Conflict model is to provide ongoing training for those assigned to lead the training effort. In reality, initial training should be completed first, before any collaborative education program is implemented. Ongoing training and facilitated feedback sessions will reinforce trainer learning and create opportunities to adapt the program to the unique elements of an organization's culture. Implementation is most effective when individuals from a variety of functions, levels, or social groups within an organization are included in the implementation team.

Conclusions

After we, as individuals and organizations, become aware of an alternative mode of interacting, we carry a tremendous responsibility. Once we realize that we can choose how we respond when we are confronted with conflict, our perceptions of conflict change and we more clearly see the shortcomings of existing models of behavior. Unfortunately, we often embody that outmoded model.

A professional colleague recently described this dilemma as it related to his career. He had been unhappy working for his employer for a number of years, and within the last year, the tensions and pressures had become intolerable. His relationship with his boss had come to be based on mutual contempt, and they each made the pain apparent. While he excelled at every other aspect of his job, he was unable to sustain an effective working relationship with his boss. They tended to communicate indirectly through e-mail and avoided interaction as much as possible. He had enlisted the help of human resources mediators and outside counseling, but it had proved ineffective for both of them. Although he had significant retirement benefits to lose, he had made up his mind that he would seek employment elsewhere. But after considerable prodding, a friend talked him into seeing one more conflict counselor.

After the third session, he returned to the office, sat down despondently, and lamented, "Before I started the sessions with this counselor, I was absolutely convinced that I wanted to quit. I was already mentally working for another company, preparing myself for the inevitable transition, but now I am totally confused.

"This counselor has really opened my eyes—after only three sessions—to what I've been doing wrong all these years. I've been completely selfish in my relationship with my boss and ignored his personal concerns in favor of business objectives. I see that now. For that matter, I see the same pattern in the relationships I have with my employees, my wife, and my kids.

"My boss isn't perfect, don't get me wrong, but now I feel this incredible weight!

"Doing the work that's required to heal these relationships is going to be exhausting, and I'm not sure I can change. And I'm not sure my boss, or the others, will trust my intentions. Quitting would certainly be the easier thing to do, but it's probably not the right thing. I don't know," he paused, "I don't know if I'm up for it."

As of this writing, seven months later, he is still working for the same company. He has described the process of resolving his conflicts as sometimes hurtful, always emotionally draining, and ever time-consuming. However, he has also said that it has been personally enriching, and although he still has a long way to go, the process has brought him closer together in his relationship with his boss. "Even if we can't resolve some of our issues," he has said, "I know the relationship has been strengthened, and we have greater understanding, acceptance, and appreciation of each other."

Listening to Conflict is a philosophy of life that guides your thoughts and behavior, and establishes principles of interaction that will help you constructively resolve the majority of the conflicts you encounter. It creates abundant solutions both inside and outside of our interactions with others. Moreover, when the conflict cannot be resolved, the principles will help you detach responsibly and walk away from the interaction at peace with the other person and with yourself.

For both individuals and organizations, the temptation to fall back into old behavior is enormous. But when you maintain discipline, desire, and patience and listen—truly, deeply, empathically listen—you will open communication channels that provide remarkable insight into the interests, needs, and criteria required for resolution. In the process, you will have facilitated an enriching relationship. When you Listen to Conflict, you build cultures of acceptance and understanding in which you are influenced and are able to influence, and in which you collaborate to seek constructive resolution.

References

Bartlett, F. C. *Remembering: An Experimental and Social Study.* Cambridge: Cambridge University Press, 1932.

Beattie, M. *Codependent No More: How to Stop Controlling Others and Start Caring for Yourself.* San Francisco: HarperSanFrancisco, HarperCollins Publishers, 1987.

Bentley, Sheila C. "Listening Better: a Guide to Improve What May Be the Ultimate Staff Skill." *Nursing Homes* 47 (February 1, 1998): 56 (3).

Bixenstine, V. E., B. Lowenfeld, and C. E. Englehart. "Role Enactment Versus Typology: Another Test of the Triangle Hypothesis." *Journal of Personality and Social Psychology* 41 (1981): 776–788.

Brehm, J. W. *A Theory of Psychological Reactance.* New York: Academic Press, 1966.

Brewer, M. B. "The Role of Ethnocentrism in Intergroup Conflict." In *The Social Psychology of Intergroup Relations,* edited by W. G. Austin and S. Worchel, 71–84. Monterey, Calif.: Brooks/Cole, 1979.

Brouwer, P. J. "The Power to See Ourselves." *Harvard Business Review* 42 (1964): 156–165.

Brown, J. D. "Evaluating One's Abilities: Shortcuts and Stumbling Blocks on the Road to Self-Knowledge." *Journal of Experimental Social Psychology* 26 (1990): 149–167.

Clore, G. L., and D. Byrne. "A Reinforcement-Affect Model of Attraction." In *Foundations of Interpersonal Attraction,* edited by T. L. Huston. New York: Academic Press, 1974.

Conway, M., and M. Ross. "Getting What You Want by Revising What You Had." *Journal of Personality and Social Psychology* 47 (1984): 738–748.

Dale, P. S. *Language Development: Structure and Function*, 2nd ed. New York: Holt, Rinehart and Winston, 1976.

Davis, J. S. "Self-Disclosure in an Acquaintance Exercise: Responsibility for Level of Intimacy." *Journal of Personality and Social Psychology* 33 (1976), 787–792.

Davis, M., and S. Franzoi. "Stability and Change in Adolescent Self-Consciousness and Empathy." *Journal of Research in Personality* 25 (1991): 70–87.

De Dreu, C. K., A. Nauta, and E. Van de Vliert. "Self-Serving Evaluations of Conflict Behavior and Escalation of the Dispute." *Journal of Applied Social Psychology* vol. 25, no. 23 (1995): 2049–2066.

Deutsch, M. "Constructive Conflict Resolution: Principles, Training, and Research." *Journal of Social Issues* 50, no. 1 (1994): 13–32.

———. "Interdependence and Psychological Orientation." In *Cooperation and Helping Behavior: Theories and Research*, edited by V. J. Derlaga and J. Grzelak, 16–43. New York: Academic Press, 1982.

———. *The Resolution of Conflict: Constructive and Destructive Processes*. New Haven, Conn.: Yale University Press, 1973.

———. "Trust and Suspicion." *Journal of Conflict Resolution* 2 (1958): 265–279.

———. "A Theory of Cooperation and Competition." *Human Relations* 2 (1949): 129–139.

de Villiers, P. A., and J. G. de Villiers. *Early Language*. Cambridge, Mass.: Harvard University Press, 1979.

Ebbesen, E. B., G. L. Kjob, and V. Konecni. "Spatial Ecology: Its Effects on the Choice of Friends and Enemies." *Journal of Experimental Social Psychology* 12 (1976): 505–518.

Egan, E. *A Skilled Helper: A Model for Systematic Helping and Interpersonal Relating*. Belmont, Calif.: Brooks/Cole, 1975.

Eisman, B., and J. Levy. "The Influence of Certain Communicative Characteristics on Lip Reading Efficiency." *Journal of Social Psychology* 51 (1960): 419–425.

Emde, R. "Mobilizing Fundamental Modes of Development:

Empathic Availability in Therapeutic Action." *Journal of American Psychoanalytic Association* 38, no. 4 (1989): 881–913.

Festinger, L., S. Schachter, and K. Back. *Social Pressures in Informal Groups: A Study of Human Factors in Housing.* New York: Harper & Row, 1950.

Fisher, R., and W. Ury. *Getting to Yes: Negotiating Agreement Without Giving In.* New York: Penguin Books, 1981.

Freud, S. *A General Introduction to Psychoanalysis.* Translated by J. Riviere. 1917. Reprint, New York: Washington Square Press, 1952.

Fromm, E. "Selfishness and Self Love." *Psychiatry* 2 (1939): 507–523.

Gibbs, N., reported by S. E. Epperson, L. Mondi, and J. L. Graff. "The EQ Factor—New Brain Research Suggests That Emotions, Not I.Q., May Be the True Measure of Human Intelligence." *Time,* 2 October 1995, 60+.

Gilligan, C. "In a Different Voice: Women's Conception of the Self and of Morality." *Harvard Educational Review* 47 (1977): 481–517.

Gladstein, G. A. "Empathy and Counseling Outcomes: An Empirical and Conceptual Review." *Counseling Psychologist* 6 (1977): 70–79.

Gottman, J. *Why Marriages Succeed or Fail.* New York: Simon & Schuster, 1994.

Hamner, W. C. "The Influence of Structural, Individual and Strategic Differences." In *Bargaining Behavior,* edited by D. L. Harnett and L. L. Cummings. Houston: Dame Publications, 1980.

Heilman, K. *Empathy: The Construct and Its Measurement.* Ann Arbor, Mich.: University Microfilms International, 1972.

Hersh, R. H., D. P. Paolitto, and J. Reimer. *Promoting Moral Growth. From Piaget to Kohlberg.* New York. Longman Inc., 1979.

Ikemi, A., and S. Kubota. "Humanistic Psychology in Japanese Corporations: Listening and the Small Steps of Change." *Journal of Humanistic Psychology* 36, no. 1 (1996): 104–121.

Johnson, D. W., and R. T. Johnson. *Cooperation and Competition: Theory and Research.* Edina, Minn.: Interaction Book Company, 1989.

Kaye, K. *Workplace Wars and How to End Them.* New York: AMA-COM, 1994.

Kelley, H. H., and D. P. Schenitzki. "Bargaining." In *Experimental Social Psychology,* edited by C. G. McClintock, 298–337. New York: Holt, Rinehart and Winston, 1972.

Kimmel, M. J., D. G. Pruitt, J. M. Magenau, E. Konar-Goldband, and P. J. D. Carnevale. "Effects of Trust Aspiration and Gender on Negotiation Tactics." Journal of Personality and Social Psychology 38 (1980): 9–23.

Lamb, M. E., and J. J. Campos. *Development in Infancy.* New York: Random House, 1982.

Levine, L. E., and M. L. Hoffman. "Empathy and Cooperation in Four-Year-Olds." *Developmental Psychology* 11 (1975): 533–534.

Lorenz, K. Z. *King Solomon's Ring: New Light on Animal Ways.* New York: Harper & Row, 1952.

Luce, R. D., and H. Raiffa. *Games and Decisions: Introduction and Critical Survey.* New York: Wiley, 1957.

Lynn, S. J. "Three Theories of Self-Disclosure." *Journal of Experimental Social Psychology* 14 (1977): 466–479.

Maslow, A. H. *Eupsychian Management.* Homewood, Ill.: Richard D. Irving and The Dorsey Press, 1965.

———. *Toward a Psychology of Being.* Princeton, N.J.: D. Von Nostrand Company, 1962.

Mayer, R. E. *The Promise of Cognitive Psychology.* San Francisco: W. H. Freeman and Company, 1981.

Moreland, R. L., and R. B. Zajonc. "Exposure Effects May Not Depend on Stimulus Recognition." *Journal of Personality and Social Psychology* 37 (1979): 1085–1096.

Morrow, L. "The Temping of America." *Time,* 29 March 1993, 40–41.

Nagel, D., M. Hoffman, and C. Hill. "A Comparison of Verbal Response Modes Used by Master's-Level Career Counselors and Other Helpers." *Journal of Counseling and Development* 74 (September/October 1995): 101–104.

Nugent, W. R., and H. Halvorson. "Testing the Effects of Active Listening." *Research on Social Work Practice* 5, no. 2 (1995): 152–175.

Ralston, F. *Hidden Dynamics.* New York: AMACOM, 1995.

Rogers, C. R. *On Becoming a Person.* Boston: Houghton Mifflin, 1961.

―――. "The Necessary and Sufficient Conditions of Therapeutic Personality Change." *Journal of Consulting Psychology* 21 (1957): 95–103.

Rokeach, M. "Some Unresolved Issues in Theories of Beliefs, Attitudes, and Values." In *1979 Nebraska Symposium on Motivation,* edited by M. M. Page. Lincoln: University of Nebraska Press, 1980.

―――. *The Nature of Human Values.* New York: Free Press, 1973.

Rosenthal, R., J. A. Hall, M. R. DiMatteo, P. L. Rogers, and D. Archer. *Sensitivity to Nonverbal Communication: The PONS Test.* (Baltimore: Johns Hopkins University Press, 1979).

Ross, M., and F. Sicoly. "Egocentric Biases in Availability and Attribution." *Journal of Personality and Social Psychology* 37 (1979): 322–336.

Rubin, J. Z. "Models of Conflict Management." *Journal of Social Issues* 50, no. 1 (1994): 33–45.

Rubin, J. Z., and B. R. Brown. *The Social Psychology of Bargaining and Negotiation.* New York: Academic Press, 1975.

Rubin, J. Z., D. G. Pruitt, and S. H. Kim. *Social Conflict: Escalation, Stalemate, and Settlement.* New York: McGraw-Hill, 1994.

Rubin, Z. "Disclosing Oneself to a Stranger: Reciprocity and Its Limits." *Journal of Experimental Social Psychology* 11 (1975): 233–260.

Schafer, R. "Generative Empathy in the Treatment Situation." *Psychiatric Quarterly* 28 (1959): 342–372.

Schank, R., and R. Abelson. *Scripts, Plans, Goals, and Understanding.* Hillsdale, N.J.: Erlbaum, 1977.

Schutz, W. C. *FIRO: A Three-Dimensional Theory of Interpersonal Behavior.* New York: Holt, Rinehart & Winston, 1958.

Scodel, A., J. S. Minas, P. Ratoosh, and M. E. Lipetz. "Some Descriptive Aspects of Two-Person and Non-Zero-Sum Games." *Journal of Conflict Resolution* 3 (1959): 114–119.

Sessa, V. "Using Perspective Taking to Manage Conflict and Affect in Teams." *Journal of Applied Behavioral Science* 32, no. 1 (1996): 101–115.

Sherif, M. *In Common Predicament: Social Psychology of Intergroup Conflict and Cooperation.* Boston: Houghton Mifflin, 1966.

Simner, M. L. "Newborn's Response to the Cry of Another Infant." *Developmental Psychology* 5 (1971): 136–150.

Skopec, E. W., and L. S. Kiely. *Everything's Negotiable.* New York: AMACOM, 1994.

Spence, G. *How to Argue and Win Every Time.* New York: St. Martin's Press, 1995.

Steil, L. K. *Your Listening Profile.* Minneapolis: Sperry Corporation, 1980.

Stevahn, L., D. Johnson, R. Johnson, and D. Real. "The Impact of a Cooperative or Individualistic Context on the Effectiveness of Conflict Resolution Training." *American Educational Research Journal* 33, no. 3 (1996): 801–823.

Suchman, J. R. "Social Sensitivity in the Small Task-Oriented Group." *Journal of Abnormal and Social Psychology* 52 (1956): 75–83.

Taylor, D. A., R. K. Gould, and P. J. Brounstein. "Effects of Personalistic Self-Disclosure." *Personality and Social Psychology Bulletin* 7 (1981): 487–492.

Tedeschi, J. T., T. Bonoma, and R. C. Brown. "A Paradigm for the Study of Coercive Power." *Journal of Conflict Resolution* 15 (1971): 197–223.

Thomas, E. J. "Effects of Facilitative Role Interdependence on Group Functioning." *Human Relations* 10 (1957): 347–366.

Tjosvold, D., and D. Johnson. "The Effects of Controversy on Cognitive Perspective-Taking." *Journal of Educational Psychology* 69 (1977): 679–685.

Thompson, L. L., and G. Lowenstein. "Egocentric Interpretations of Fairness and Interpersonal Conflict." *Organization Behavior and Human Decision Processes* 51 (1992): 176–197.

———. "From Self-Serving Evaluations of Conflict Behavior and Escalation of the Dispute."

Weinberger, D. A. "The Construct Validity of the Repressive Coping Style." In *Repression and Dissociation,* edited by J. L. Singer. Chicago: University of Chicago Press, 1990.

Wispe, L. G. "Sympathy and Empathy." In *International Encyclopedia of the Social Sciences,* edited by D. L. Sills. Vol. 15. New York: Macmillan, 1968.

Index